Walk Around

MiG-21 Fishbed

By Hans-Heiri Stapfer

Color by Don Greer and David Gebhardt

Illustrated by Darren Glenn

Part 2

Walk Around Number 39

squadron/signal publications

Introduction

The Mikoyan-Gurevich Design Bureau developed the third generation MiG-21 variants to give the Fishbed (the MiG-21's North Atlantic Treaty Organization – NATO – code name) a further increase in both range and weapons load. This was largely due to criticisms levelled at earlier generation Fishbeds flown in combat during the Vietnam and the Middle Eastern wars.

The **MiG-21S** (*Sapfir*; Sapphire) (Fishbed J) was the first third generation interceptor/air superiority fighter. This aircraft was powered by a 13,668-pound thrust Tumansky R-11-F2S-300 afterburning turbojet engine. The MiG-21S was equipped with the new RP-22S *Sapfir* 21 (NATO code name Jay Bird) radar. The MiG-21S was built exclusively for the *Voenno Vozdushnye Sili* (VVS; Soviet Air Force) at *Gosudarstvenny Aviatsionny Zavod* (GAZ; State Aircraft Factory) 21 at Gorky (now Nizhny-Novgorod) between 1965 and 1968.

The **MiG-21SM** (*Modifikatsirovanny*; Modified) (Fishbed J) was an improved MiG-21S with an uprated 14,308-pound thrust Tumansky R-13-300 powerplant and a semi-internal 23мм GSh-23L cannon with 200 rounds mounted on the fuselage centerline. It was the first Fishbed variant equipped with four wing pylons. GAZ 21 produced the MiG-21SM for the VVS between 1968 and 1974.

The **MiG-21M** (Fishbed J) was the MiG-21SM's export version, which was powered by the earlier R-11-F2S-300 engine of the MiG-21S. Additionally, the RP-21MA (Spin Scan) radar was installed in place of the MiG-21SM's later RP-22S *Sapfir* 21. MiG-21Ms were also equipped with the ASP-PFD gun sight. Improved R-11-F2SK-300s powered late production MiG-21Ms. The MiG-21M was built at GAZ 30 '*Znamya Truda*' (Banner of Labor), located at Moscow-Khodinka, between 1968 and 1971. The **MiG-21MF** (*Forsirovanny*; Boosted) (Fishbed J) satisfied the needs of various export customers for an uprated MiG-21M. The MiG-21MF was equipped with the MiG-21SM's Tumansky R-13-300 engine and RP-22S *Sapfir* 21 radar. The MiG-21MF was built for the VVS at GAZ 21 and for export at GAZ 30 between 1970 and 1975.

The **MiG-21MF/RNAV** was a post-Communist Czech modification of their MiG-21MF fleet to make this type NATO compatible. The Czechs modified ten Fishbed Js to this standard for the 21. *Základna Taktického Letectva* (ZTL; Tactical Air Base) at Caslav.

The **MiG-21bis Lazur** (Azure beam-beacon receiver) (Fishbed L) was the first fourth generation Fishbed variant. It was mostly a complete redesign of the Fishbed. Lighter weight titanium airframe components replaced most steel airframe components. The MiG-21bis was equipped with the RP-22SMA *Sapfir* radar, which provided the Fishbed L with a limited lookdown shoot-down capacity. Cockpit instrumentation and many avionics from the MiG-23 (Flogger) were also incorporated into the MiG-21bis Lazur. A 15,635-pound thrust Tumansky R-25-300 turbojet with an improved afterburner system powered the Fishbed L. The first MiG-21bis Lazurs were delivered to the VVS in February of 1972.

The **MiG-21bis SAU** (Fishbed N) was the ultimate Fishbed variant. (SAU referred to the Autopilot.) It was externally distinguished from the earlier MiG-21bis Lazur by the additional RSBN-2S (Swift Rod) Instrument Landing System (ILS) antennas under the air intake and above the rudder. GAZ 21 built the last MiG-21bis SAU in 1982.

Acknowledgements

A number of fellow friends and organizations had contributed to this Walk Around. I express my sincere thanks to a number of people that had assisted me in writing this volume:

Jozef And'al	Werner Greppmeir	Hans Schreiber
Armeemuseum der DDR	Kerstin Gutbrod	Roman Sekyrka
Detlef Billig	Zdenek Hurt	Sergej F. Sergejev
Robert Bock	Paul A. Jackson	Peter Steinemann
Stephan Boshniakov	Helmut Kluger	Wolfgang Tamme
Amelia Cachay	Lubomir Kudlicka	Pavel Türk
Dick Cole	Wojciech Luczak	Hans-Georg Volprich
Croatian Ministry of Defense	Hans-Joachim Mau (†)	Nicholas J. Waters III
Deutsches Museum – Werft	Andrzej Morgala	Simon Watson
Schleissheim	Michal Ovcacik	Harald Ziewe
Jaroslav Farkas	George Petkov	Andrej Zinchuk
JaPo Collection	G.F. Petrov	4+ Publications
Gerhard Filchner	Tomas Poruba	
Marcus Fülber	Eckhardt Prell	

All photographs were taken by the author unless otherwise credited.

COPYRIGHT 2005 SQUADRON/SIGNAL PUBLICATIONS, INC.

1115 CROWLEY DRIVE CARROLLTON, TEXAS 75011-5010

ISBN 0-89747-486-4

If you have any photographs of aircraft, armor, soldiers or ships of any nation, particularly wartime snapshots, why not share them with us and help make Squadron/Signal's books all the more interesting and complete in the future. Any photograph sent to us will be copied and the original returned. The donor will be fully credited for any photos used. Please send them to:

Squadron/Signal Publications, Inc.
1115 Crowley Drive
Carrollton, TX 75011-5010

Если у вас есть фотографии самолётов, вооружения, солдат или кораблей любой страны, особенно, снимки времён войны, поделитесь с нами и помогите сделать новые книги издательства Эскадрон/Сигнал ещё интереснее. Мы переснимем ваши фотографии и вернём оригиналы. Имена приславших снимки будут сопровождать все опубликованные фотографии. Пожалуйста, присылайте фотографии по адресу:

Squadron/Signal Publications, Inc.
1115 Crowley Drive
Carrollton, TX 75011-5010

軍用機、装甲車両、兵士、軍艦などの写真を 所持しておられる方は いらっしゃいませんか？どの国のものでも結構です。作戦中に撮影されたものが特に良いのです。Squadron/Signal社の出版する刊行物において、このような写真は内容を一層充実し、興味深くすることができます。当方にお送り頂いた写真は、複写の後お返しいたします。出版物中に写真を使用した場合は、必ず提供者のお名前を明記させて頂きます。お写真は下記にご送付ください。

Squadron/Signal Publications, Inc.
1115 Crowley Drive
Carrollton, TX 75011-5010

(Front Cover) This MiG-21*bis Lazur* (17) was assigned to the 115th Guards Fighter Aviation Regiment. This unit was deployed to Afghanistan during the 1979-88 Soviet-Afghan War. SOVIETSKAYA LITVA (SOVIET LITHUANIA) is painted on the nose, while the Guards insignia appears under the canopy.

(Previous Page) This MiG-21*bis Lazur* is assigned to the 21. *Eskadrila Lovackih Zrakoplova* (ELZ; Fighter Aviation Squadron), *Hratsko Ratno Zrakoplovstvo* (HRZ; Croatian Air Force). The Squadron's insignia is painted on the nose, but there is no tactical number on the aircraft. The 21. ELZ is based at Pleso Air Base near Zagreb, Croatia's capital. (Croatian Ministry of Defense)

(Back Cover) A Taliban-flown MiG-21*bis Lazur* (White 978) flies from Bagram Air Base, Afghanistan in January of 2001. It was accompanying another Fishbed L on a mission against United Front strongpoints in northeast Afghanistan's Takhar province. This MiG-21*bis Lazur* was previously Red 978 while flown by the pro-Soviet Afghan Air Force.

MiG-21SM/M (Fishbed J)

The MiG-21SM (Soviet Air Force) and MiG-21M (export version) were externally identical. These Fishbeds were the first equipped with the 23ᴍᴍ GSh-23L cannon and four wing pylons. MiG-21SM/Ms lacked the rear view mirror atop the canopy and the gas deflector plates below the forward fuselage airflow relief doors.

MiG-21M/SM (Modified) (Fishbed J)

During its operational service, several MiG-21SM and MiG-21Ms were refitted with gun gas deflector plates below the airflow relief doors. These gas deflector plates became standard on the MiG-21MF.

MiG-21MF (Fishbed J)

MiG-21MFs were distinguished from the earlier MiG-21SM/M versions by the TS-27AMSh rear view mirror mounted atop the canopy. Several MiG-21SM/Ms were also modified this way, making them externally indistinguishable from the MiG-21MF. Some export MiG-21Ms were also retrofitted with the MiG-21MF's more powerful 14,308-pound Tumansky R-13-300 engine during a general overhaul.

MiG-21*bis Lazur* (Fishbed L)

The MiG-21*bis Lazur* featured a wider, deeper dorsal spine than the earlier MiG-21MF. This spine was faired further back into the vertical fin, nearly to the braking parachute bullet fairing.

MiG-21*bis* SAU (Fishbed N)

The MiG-21*bis* SAU was distinguished from the earlier MiG-21*bis Lazur* in having additional RSBN-2S (NATO designation Swift Rod) Instrument Landing System (ILS) antennas mounted under the air intake and atop the tailfin.

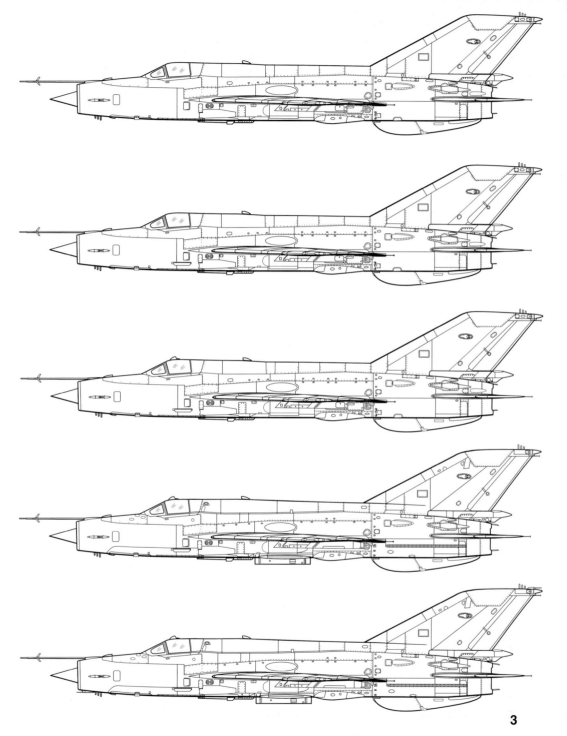

(Above) The MiG-21M (Fishbed J) was an export version based on the MiG-21SM. The MiG-21M was equipped with the older RP-21MA radar instead of the MiG-21SM's more sophisticated RP-22S *Sapfir* (Sapphire) 21 radar. Most cockpit instruments and avionics were taken from the earlier MiG-21PFM (Fishbed F). A gun gas deflector plate is mounted on the lower forward fuselage below the air-flow relief door. All MiG-21Ms left *Gosudarstvenny Aviatsionny Zavod* (GAZ; State Aircraft Factory) 30 *'Znamya Truda'* (Banner of Labor) at Moscow-Khodinka without this plate, which was retrofitted during a general overhaul. This MiG-21M (Serial Number 3302) once served as Red 493 in the *Luftstreitkräfte der Nationalen Volksarmee* (LSK NVA; East German Air Force). After the 1990 unification of East and West Germany, the *Bundesluftwaffe* (Federal German Air Force) assigned it the inventory registration 22+59. This Fishbed J was scrapped at Dresden, Germany on 29 September 1992. (Marcus Fülber)

(Left) MiG-21Ms served with many air forces in the Soviet Union's sphere of influence. This *Silakh al-Jawwiya as-Sudaniya* (Sudanese Air Force) MiG-21M (Black 344) participated in BRIGHT STAR '83. This was a US-Egyptian military exercise held in Egypt during August of 1983. The tactical number painted on the nose and the rear fuselage was applied in both Arabic and English style digits. An APU-13 missile launch rail was mounted on the outer wing pylon. APU-13s were used to carry R-3S (AA-2 Atoll) Infrared (IR) homing Air-to-Air Missiles (AAMs) (US Department of Defense)

(Above) The MiG-21SM/M introduced the DVA-3A Angle of Attack (AoA) sensor on the left side of the nose. Additionally, the PVD-7 air data boom was moved from the upper center nose on the earlier MiG-21PFM (Fishbed F) to the right side on the Fishbed J. This MiG-21M (White 613/Serial Number 960613) was flown by the *Bulgarski Voyenno Vozdushni Sili* (BVVS; Bulgarian Air Force). It is displayed at the Air and Space Museum located at Krumovo Air Base near Plovdiv, Bulgaria.

(Above Right) The DVA-3A AoA sensor only appeared on the left nose of the MiG-21S/SM/M and subsequent variants. This sensor was connected with the AP-155 three-axis (pitch, roll, and yaw) autopilot. Earlier MiG-21 variants lacked the AP-155 and therefore did not have the DVA-3A AoA sensor.

(Right) A distinctive feature on MiG-21S/SM/Ms was the lack of gun gas deflector plates below the left and right airflow relief doors. Later MiG-21MF (Fishbed J) and MiG-21*bis* (Fishbed L/N) variants were equipped with these plates. Many MiG-21S/SM/Ms were subsequently retrofitted with deflector plates, which made them externally indistinguishable from the MiG-21MF and MiG-21*bis* variants. Some early MiG-21PFs (Fishbed D) and MiG-21PFMs (Fishbed F) were also retrofitted with gun gas deflector plates during overhauls. (See SS5537 MiG-21 Fishbed Walk Around, Part 1 from squadron/signal publications.)

Polish pilots perform a pre-flight check in front of a MiG-21M (Red 1903/Serial Number 961903). Each pilots wears a GSh-6 helmet. The 23MM GSh-23L two-barreled cannon and no gun gas deflector plate below the airflow relief door clearly identify this Fishbed J as a MiG-21M. The earlier MiG-21PFM did not carry the semi-internal GSh-23L. (WAF)

A BVVS MiG-21M (Red 209/Serial Number 960209) is prepared for a mission. This Fishbed J was delivered to Bulgaria in August of 1969 and was assigned to the 19. IAP at Graf Ignatievo, near Plovdiv. The BVVS phased out the Fishbed J in 1990. A wire connecting the two airflow relief door covers ensured that all coverings had been removed from the airflow relief doors before a mission. Leaving a covering on the aircraft can cause an engine flame out during take off. (Stephan Boshniakov)

The MiG-21M lacked the canopy mounted rear view mirror, but was fitted with the DVA-3A AoA indicator. Red coverings protected the air intake, the boundary layer exhaust port, and the DVA-3A AoA indicator. This BVVS (Bulgarian Air Force) MiG-21M (Red 714/Serial Number 960714) has 68+18 painted on the front airflow relief door. This Fishbed was delivered to the 19. *Iztrebitelen Aviazionen Polk* (IAP; Fighter Aviation Regiment) during August of 1969 and crashed on 26 August 1974. (Stephan Boshniakov)

A pre-flight check is made on an LSK NVA (East German Air Force) MiG-21M (Red 553/Serial Number 0407). This aircraft later received the *Bundesluftwaffe* (Federal German Air Force) inventory number 22+80. The three stars in the winged Q and one above it meant this MiG-21M had won the *Flugzeug der ausgezeichneten Qualität* (Aircraft in Excellent Condition) award in five inspections. (The stars symbolized repeat awards.) This Fishbed J's cockpit section is now exhibited at the *Technik Museum* (Technical Museum) in Speyer, Germany; however, the rest of the airframe was scrapped. (Hans-Joachim Mau)

Romanian pilots scramble to their MiG-21Ms. All pilots wear the green VKK-6 high altitude flying suit and the GSh-6M helmet. This helmet had to be connected with the VKK-6 before the pilot entered the Fishbed. The uncomfortable VKK-6 flying suits were only worn on high altitude missions and were generally disliked by flying crews. (WAF)

Bulgarian flight and ground crews pose in front of a 19. IAP MiG-21M. The aircraft on the right has a UB-16-57U pod on the inboard wing pylon. This pod held sixteen 57mm S-5 unguided rockets. The UB-16-57U was quickly replaced by the 32-tube UB-32A pod on the MiG-21M. The pilot wears a ZSh-3 helmet, while the ground crewman on the right wears sandals instead of ordnance shoes. (Stephan Boshniakov)

A Polish pilot helps his comrade exit from a MiG-21M (Red 1008). Both pilots wear the standard day fighter pilot suit, which was much more comfortable than the VKK-6 high altitude flying suit initially worn by MiG-21SM/M pilots. The VVS (Soviet Air Force) and most Warsaw Pact (WARPAC) countries used this type of crew access ladder. The tactical number 1008 was repeated on both the airflow relief door cover and the 490 L (129-gallon) centerline fuel tank. (WAF)

7

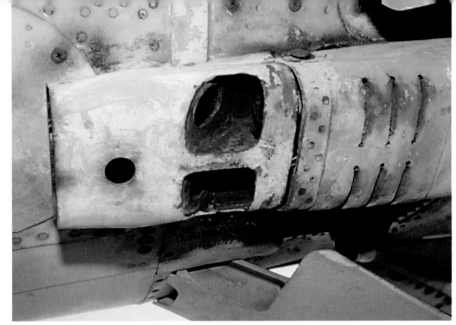

The 23mm Gryasev-Shipunov GSh-23L twin-barreled cannon's muzzle is parallel with the fuselage centerline. The MiG-21SM/M was the first Fishbed variant equipped with this semi-internal weapon, although earlier MiG-21PF/PFMs could carry this weapon in a GP-9 pack on the centerline. The GSh-23L has a muzzle velocity of 735 m (2411 feet) per second.

The ammunition access panel is mounted above the GSh-23L's starboard side. This louvered panel was opened to load 23mm ammunition belts into the cannon. Circular apertures are found on the GSh-23L fairing. This cannon is 153.7 cm (60.5 inches) long.

The muzzle of the 23mm GSh-23L cannon on a MiG-21M is viewed from below. Apertures in the barrels' covering allowed gun gases to exit from the fairing. Both forward speed brakes flanked the GSh-23L when they were deployed.

Spent cases were ejected through the splayed chutes mounted on both cannon fairing sides. The 52 kg (115-pound) GSh-23L cannon was developed based on the Gast principle first employed in Germany in 1916. One barrel's recoil automatically loaded and fired the other barrel. The gun's centerline position minimized negative recoil force effects on the airframe.

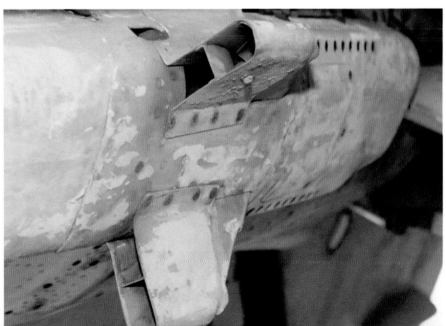

The GSh-23L's right rear fairing formed part of the fuselage and wing root. This was also the case with the left rear fairing. Inlets placed in this fairing brought cooling air into the cannon's mechanism. The louvered panel was removed for rearming the cannon. A well-trained ground crew could reload the MiG-21M's GSh-23L within ten minutes.

Spent ammunition cases were ejected through the rear of the chutes splayed from the cannon fairing. The two-barreled GSh-23L has an impressive firing rate of 3000 to 3400 rounds per minute. This weapon also armed the MiG-23 (Flogger) fighter and was mounted in the tail turrets of Tupolev Tu-22M-3 (Backfire C) and Tu-95MS (Bear H) bombers.

The GSh-23L's rear fairing was removed for servicing the weapon. Soviet aircraft weapons and systems were designed for ease of maintenance. Most Soviet aircraft mechanics were conscripts that were supervised by a core of professional mechanics.

The MiG-21M lacked the TS-27AMSh rear view mirror atop the canopy. This was typical for MiG-21SM/M variants. The outlets just below the fuselage spine were only introduced on the right fuselage side, but not on the left.

Early third generation Fishbeds did not have the TS-27AMSh rear view mirror as production standard. This was also the case on the MiG-21R (Fishbed H) reconnaissance variant, which was based on the MiG-21S airframe.

This *Al Quwwat al-Jawwia il-Misriya* (Egyptian Air Force) MiG-21M (Black 8212) was retrofitted with a TS-27AMSh rear view mirror. The mirror became standard on the MiG-21MF. Introduction of the TS-27AMSh resulted in deletion of the two small rear view mirrors mounted on the canopy frame. The MiG-21M lacked the gun gas deflector plates below the left and right airflow relief doors. The tactical number was painted in Black on the second Medium Green (dark) band from the nose. (Dick Cole/Cole Aero Graphics)

A small inlet was installed just aft of the canopy. This inlet was only fitted to the MiG-21SM/M's left side, but never on the right side. Air fed through this inlet cooled avionics (aviation electronics) located within this section of the fuselage. Flush-mounted screws were used to fasten various access panels to the airframe. The stud projecting from the aft canopy frame is believed to fit inside a canopy cover eye. This cover protected the windshield and canopy while the aircraft is parked outdoors.

Two LSK NVA (East German Air Force) natural metal MiG-21Ms and one MiG-21UM (Mongol B) trainer undergo overhaul. Large vinyl tarpaulins placed over the wing upper surfaces prevented damage to the aircraft. The MiG-21M in the center was retrofitted with gun gas deflector plates on both sides. Access panels on the dorsal fairing were removed from the two MiG-21Ms. These panels aft of the cockpit were opened for servicing the AP-155 autopilot. Both Fishbed Js were jacked up for inspection. An aircraft silhouette is painted on the floor below each MiG-21. This is believed to indicate the aircraft's position within the hangar for efficient maintenance operation. (Hans-Joachim Mau)

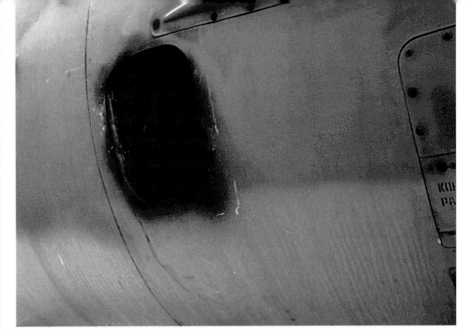

Lack of the gun gas deflector plate below the airflow relief door is typical for the MiG-21SM/M versions. The external power outlet is located just below the left wing root fairing on this Bulgarian MiG-21M.

The MiG-21M's external power receptacle was located just above the left fuselage speed brake. The covering for the 115 Volt/400 Herz Alternating Current (AC) power (right) is missing, while the covering for the 27 Volt Direct Current (DC) power (left) is still attached to this Bulgarian MiG-21M. Electrical power for aircraft systems was supplied through this receptacle prior to take off.

An airflow relief door is mounted on the left side of this MiG-21M. An identical door is located on the right side. These relief doors opened for additional airflow into the engine during take off.

This triangle was painted on all *Bulgarski Voyenno Vozdushni Sili* (BVVS; Bulgarian Air Force) aircraft since the 1930s. The marking is located just below the MiG-21M's wing root fairing. The upper number 96 in the triangle is the MiG-21M's inventory number of the type, while the lower number 0613 is the aircraft's Bulgarian serial number. Bulgaria was the only former WARPAC country to employ this inventory system.

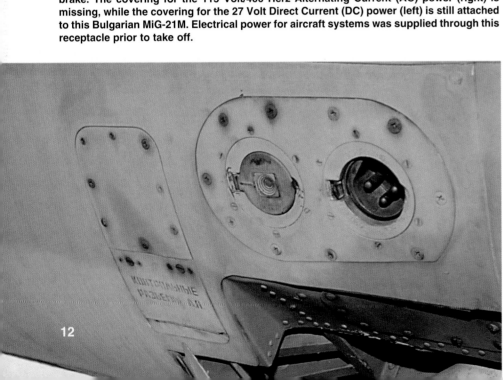

(Above) The opened canopy reveals the cockpit of an *Al Quwwat al-Jawwia il-Misriya* (Egyptian Air Force) MiG-21M (Black 8212). This Fishbed J participated in the US-Egyptian exercise BRIGHT STAR 83 held in Egypt during August of 1983. The MiG-21M was the downgraded export version of the MiG-21SM, which only saw service within the *Voenno Vozdushnye Sili* (VVS: Soviet Air Force). Most of the MiG-21M's cockpit instruments and equipment were taken from the previous MiG-21PFM (Fishbed F) variant. The MiG-21M was equipped with an RP-21MA (NATO designation Spin Scan) radar, instead of the newer RP-22MS *Sapfir* 21 (NATO designation Jay Bird) mounted on the MiG-21SM. (Dick Cole/Cole Aero Graphics)

(Right) The cockpit is exposed on a *Luftstreitkräfte der Nationalen Volksarmee* (LSK NVA; East German Air Force) MiG-21M (Red 611/Serial Number 1111). This aircraft was delivered to East Germany in August of 1969 and assigned to *Jagdfliegergeschwader* (JG; Fighter Aviation Regiment) 7 'Wilhelm Pieck' at Drewitz. It was originally intended for delivery to another country and was delivered to East Germany with English language airframe inscriptions (stenciling) and English written operational manuals. The Brown-Red colored leather seat was not standard. An altimeter was installed above the SSh-45-100OS gun camera, which is located to the left of the ASP-PFD optical gun sight. This is a non-standard feature, since most Fishbed Js had the Angle of Attack (AoA) indicator located in this position. The gun sight's position above the instrument panel is a distinctive feature for the MiG-21M. Earlier MiG-21PFMs had the gun sight mounted atop the windshield frame. (Marcus Fülber)

13

Full deployment of the MiG-21M's left speed brake exposes the shallow speed brake bay. This brake was actuated using a hydraulic jack mounted in the bay's front section. These speed brakes were similar to those in previous MiG-21 variants. All Fishbeds employed three speed brakes – two forward, one aft – to maintain the aircraft's trim in flight during brake deployment.

The centerline mounted aft speed brake is deployed on a BVVS MiG-21M. This brake had a maximum deflection angle of 40°. This speed brake could not be lowered when the 490 L (129-gallon) fuel tank was installed on the centerline pylon; however, the forward brakes could deploy when the centerline tank was mounted.

The left speed brake is deployed on this *Bulgarski Voyenno Vozdushni Sili* (BVVS: Bulgarian Air Force) MiG-21M. Both forward (left and right) brakes had a maximum deflection angle of 35°. These brakes operated in unison with the aft fuselage speed brake. All MiG-21 speed brakes were hydraulically actuated.

This *Letectvo Ceskoslovenske Lidove Armady* (LCLA; Czechoslovak People's Army Air Force) MiG-21M (Black 1114) is prepared for another training flight. Red coverings over the airflow relief doors kept Foreign Object Damage (FOD) out of these orifices. This Fishbed J lacked the gun gas deflector plates below the relief doors and the TS-27AMSh rear view mirror atop the canopy early in its service life. *Gosudarstvenny Aviatsionny Zavod* (GAZ; State Aircraft Factory) 30 *'Znamya Truda'* (Banner of Labor) at Moscow-Khodinka delivered the MiG-21M in this configuration. (Zdenek Hurt)

During its operational service, most MiG-21Ms delivered to WARPAC countries were retrofitted with a gas deflector plate below each airflow relief door and the TS-27AMSh rear view mirror. These modifications made the MiG-21M externally identical to the MiG-21MF. This same MiG-21M (Black 1114) received these modifications during its LCLA operational service. (Sign via Roman Sekyrka)

The Bulgarian MiG-21M's aft centerline speed brake is fully extended at 40°. The centerline fuselage pylon's aft section is located immediately in front of the speed brake. Circular openings reduced buffeting when the brake was deployed and were a typical Fishbed speed brake feature.

(Above Left) A well-weathered *Letectvo Ceskoslovenske Armady* (LCA; Czechoslovak Army Air Force) MiG-21MF (Black 7803) has fully deployed its three speed brakes just prior to landing. No centerline fuel tank is carried, which enables the Fishbed J to extend the aft brake. This was not possible when the 490 ʟ tank was mounted on the centerline pylon. Czechoslovakia's Air Force was renamed the *Letectvo Ceskoslovenske Armady* in January of 1990, after the Communist government's fall. On 1 January 1993, Czechoslovakia's split into the Czech Republic and Slovakia resulted in the LCA being renamed the *Letectvo Armady Ceske* (LAC; Czech Army Air Force). (Sign via Roman Sekyrka)

(Above) An LSK NVA (East German Air Force) pilot stands beside a MiG-21MF (Red 427/Serial Number 7603) prior to a mission. A Red cockpit access ladder is placed by the fuselage. This Fishbed J was originally assigned to *Jagdfliegergeschwader* (JG; Fighter Aviation Regiment) 8 *'Hermann Matern'* at Marxwalde on 18 March 1972. It was later reassigned to JG 3 *'Wladimir Komarow'* at Preschen and finally to JG 1 *'Fritz Schmenkel'* at Holzdorf. The West Germans assigned the inventory number 23+03 to this MiG-21MF before it was scrapped at Dresden on 14 September 1993.

(Left) Two LAC MiG-21MFs (White 7701 and White 7711) fly formation with a MiG-21UM trainer (Yellow 3756) in the lead. These MiG-21s were assigned to the LAC's *Stressova Letka* (Stress Squadron), a trials and demonstration unit at Caslav. White 7711 retained its original camouflage, but White 7701 was painted overall Black. The White-Red-Blue upper fuselage stripes represent the Czech Republic's national colors. White 7711 and Yellow 3756 both crashed after a mid-air collision on 8 June 1998. (Jan Kouba via Lubomir Kudlicka)

(Above) This MiG-21MF (Black 201) was one of approximately 12 Fishbed Js delivered to the *Bangladesh Biman Bahini* (BBB; Bangladesh Air Force). No ordnance or missile rails are carried on the wing pylons. The serial number 7201 was painted in Black below the fin flash on the vertical stabilizer (tailfin). The tactical number 201 was originally painted in smaller numbers on this MiG-21MF's nose. (Peter Steinemann)

(Above Right) A special marking is painted on this *Polskie Wojska Lotnicze* (PWL; Polish Air Force) MiG-21MF (Red 6814/Serial Number 966814). This marking resembles the Fishbed, which was the Air Standards Coordinating Committee (ASCC) reporting name for the MiG-21 fighter variants. The North Atlantic Treaty Organization (NATO) established the ASCC in 1954. This Committee assigned easy to distinguish code names for Soviet aircraft and missiles believed to be in service. Fighters received code names beginning with F, bombers' names began with B, cargo aircraft names started with C, helicopters had H names, and miscellaneous aircraft (including trainers) employed code names starting with M. (Marcus Fülber)

(Right) A MiG-21MF (C1495) is nearest in a formation of various *Bharatiya Vayu Sena* (BVS; Indian Air Force) MiG fighters. A MiG-25R flies lead, with a MiG-23MF (left) and MiG-23BN just aft. A MiG-29 flies opposite of the MiG-21MF. The Fishbed J was assigned to No. 30 'Vultures' Squadron at Tezpur, India. This Squadron's insignia appears on the nose, just in front of the Saffron (center), White, and Green national marking. An additional radio antenna is mounted beside the MiG-21MF's nose boom. Green discs were painted on the tail for Air Combat Maneuvering (ACM) training. (Peter Steinemann)

17

The MiG-21MF's dielectric nose cone was made of laminated wood and covered with a plastic foil. Wood is a dielectric material that easily allows radar waves to pass through it. Most third and fourth generation MiG-21s had radomes painted Radome Green (FS24108). This exact shade differed slightly among manufacturers. This MiG-21MF is exhibited at the *Deutsches Museum – Werft Schlessheim* (German Museum – Schleissheim Workshop).

Most of the radome was made from laminated wood and covered with a plastic foil; however, the tip was made of metal. This is believed to be due to the increased heat and aerodynamic stress of this radome section at high-speed flight. MiG-21SM/M and MiG-21MF radomes were identical.

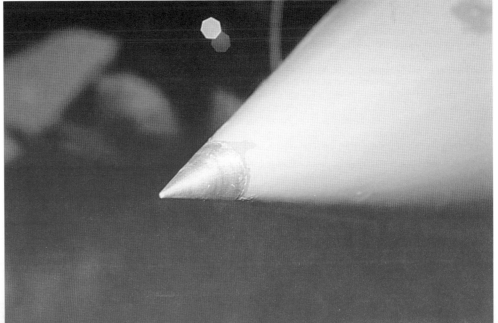

The MiG-21MF's conical radome was mounted within the engine air intake. The RP-22S *Sapfir* 21 radar (NATO designation Jay Bird) had a conventional dish antenna, which moved inside the dielectric nose cone. Dielectric materials do not conduct electricity, including radar waves. Electronics are cooled by boundary layer air diverged (branched off) by the ring surrounding the nose cone. The MiG-21PFM's center mounted PVD-7 air data boom was repositioned to the right on the MiG-21SM/M/MFs. (Harald Ziewe)

The plastic air intake cover was painted Red on most third and fourth generation MiG-21s. This cover prevented FOD from entering the intake and damage to the radome. Most of the coverings had the aircraft's tactical number painted on it to prevent unauthorized 'borrowing.' A BVVS (Bulgarian Air Force) Lisunov Li-2 transport is parked behind this MiG-21MF.

The Angle of Attack (AoA) sensor was only mounted on the MiG-21MF's left nose. The DVA-3A AoA indicator was introduced with the AP-155 autopilot. Earlier MiG-21PFMs lacked both the AP-155 and the DVA-3A. The AoA sensor was identical on both the MiG-21SM/M and MiG-21MF.

Mechanics perform an engine check on a Light Gray *Letectvo Ceskoslovenske Lidove Armady* (LCLA; Czechoslovak People's Army Air Force) MiG-21MF (Black 4003). A protective cage was wheeled before the air intake to prevent the R-13-F-300 engine from ingesting debris. Two metal cables connected the main landing gear to hooks in the ramp. These cables were employed during engine checks, since the Fishbed J's brakes were insufficient to hold the aircraft in place. (Zdenek Hurt)

The AoA sensor feeds inputs to both the AP-155 autopilot and the DVA-3A AoA indicator. The DVA-3A warns the pilot if the aircraft is stalling with two Red lights on the instrument panel and an audible alarm.

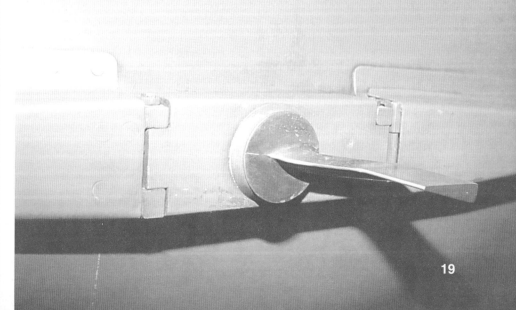

The RP-22S *Sapfir* (Sapphire) 21 radar (NATO designation Jay Bird) weighs 140 KG (309 pounds). The Volkov *Konstruktorskoe Byuro* (KB; Design Bureau) developed this radar system. The RP-22S *Sapfir* 21 has an effective tail-on pursuit range of 15 KM (9.3 miles). The MiG-21MF was the first Fishbed J export variant equipped with the RP-22S *Sapfir* 21.

Earlier MiG-21Ms were fitted with the older RP-21MA (Spin Scan) radar, while Soviet MiG-21S/SMs had the RP-22S. Openings cut into the radome of this former East German Fishbed J reveal the dish antenna. This radome with radar set is now displayed at the *Deutsches Museum – Werft Schleissheim*.

A covering protects the RP-22S *Sapfir* 21 radar system's dish antenna. The entire radar slides hydraulically aft and forward with the radome, according to the flight conditions. A hydraulic actuator system moved the radome to increase or decrease the amount of airflow into the intake in response to flight conditions.

The RP-22S *Sapfir* 21 relied heavily on 1960s electronic technology. This system employed at least 150 vacuum tubes (thermionic valves) when contemporary Western radars employed solid-state (semiconductor) electronics. The RP-22S had the same dimensions as the earlier RP-21, but the former's greater power gave the RP-22S an enhanced range.

The RP-22S *Sapfir* 21 radar's dish antenna is exposed through an opening cut in the covering. This system employed a single antenna for search and track modes. Early Soviet radars had separate antennas for these two modes.

21

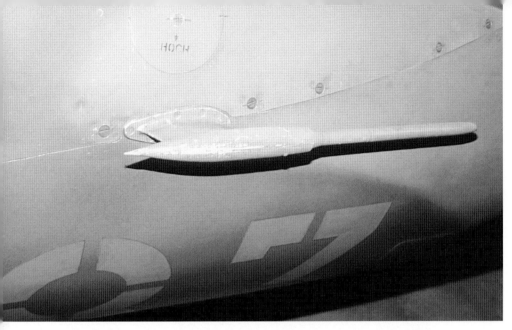

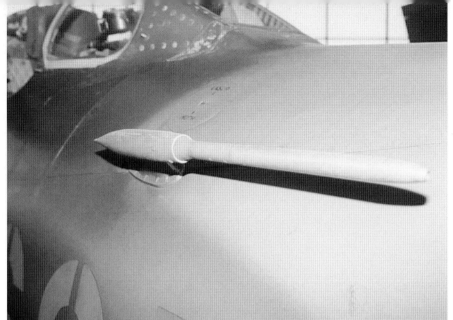

An auxiliary air pressure tube was mounted on the right side of the MiG-21MF's forward fuselage. This tube collected dynamic air pressure for the flight control system's q-feel. This synthetic feel resembled the natural response from aerodynamic loads, which made it approximately proportional to dynamic pressure. The tube's position was away from the airflow immediately around the airframe, which would result in inaccurate readings.

This platform held the MiG-21MF's auxiliary air pressure tube. Screws fixed the tube to the right nose section. This tube was removed for servicing when required. This streamlined fairing reduced the drag imposed by this tube's presence away from the forward fuselage.

The MiG-21MF and the earlier MiG-21SM/M all received an auxiliary air pressure tube with a long boom. The earlier MiG-21PFM and MiG-21S lacked this boom on the TP-156M auxiliary air pressure tube.

A 4 L (1.1-gallon) bottle of pure alcohol was placed within this panel immediately ahead of the MiG-21MF's windshield. Alcohol for de-icing the windshield was sprayed using pressurized air. Boundary air collected in the engine intake exited from the aircraft through this vent. The PVD-7 air data boom's rear section is located to the panel's right.

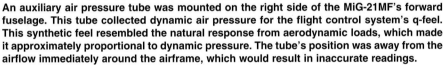

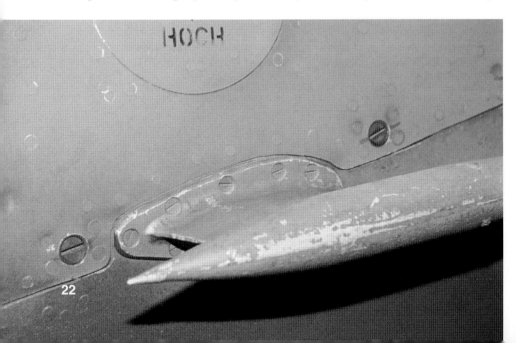

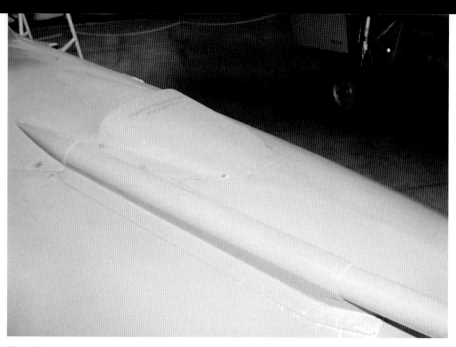

The PVD-7 air data boom's rear section faired into the MiG-21MF's upper right nose. The de-icing alcohol bottle is located within the fairing on the upper nose center.

The MiG-21MF's PVD-7 air data boom was equipped with precision air data sensors. These sensors worked with the *Pion-N* (Peony-N) feeder device to sense dynamic pressure. This boom also had three static pressure ports and pairs of angular measures of angle of attack (forward vanes) and yaw (aft vanes). Input from the freely pivoted swept-back vanes helped reduce engine stalls, but this was primarily required to assist gun aiming. These sensors were introduced on the MiG-21SM/M variants. Previous MiG-21PF/PFM variants lacked these sensors on the data boom.

The PVD-7 air data boom platform is mounted on the right nose section. This identical boom was used on both the MiG-21SM/M and the MiG-21MF. A plate that formed the forward edge of the boom platform diverted air to the left or right of the aircraft's surface.

Precision air data sensors are mounted in the PVD-7 air data boom. The boom's front section was left unpainted and was heated to prevent icing. This feature was found on all operational MiG-21SM/Ms and MiG-21MFs. Air data vanes are mounted aft of the boom's tip.

23

The MiG-21MF's nose landing gear employed one wheel that was connected to a main gear strut. This KT-102 (*Koleso Tarmaznoye*; Braked Wheel) nose wheel with tire was 500ᴍᴍ (19.7 inches) in diameter by 180ᴍᴍ (7.1 inches) wide. The pressurized feed line to the multi disc brake runs down the gear strut to the wheel's right side. This wheel is painted Blue-Green (approximately FS25193).

Pressurized air for the KT-102 nose wheel's brakes was fed through a hose that ran down the nose gear strut's left side. The UA-24 anti-skid sensor was only mounted on the left side of the rim. MiG-21SM/Ms and MiG-21MFs employed the same nose wheel. In case of an emergency, the front gear leg can be either lowered manually or with the help of pressurized air.

The steerable KT-102 nose wheel hydraulically retracted forward into the nose wheel well. The nose wheel strut's hydraulic cylinder is clearly visible. The KT-102 nose wheel is equipped with a hydro-pneumatic damper that reduced vibration. Various electrical cables and hydraulic and pneumatic pipes run through the nose wheel well.

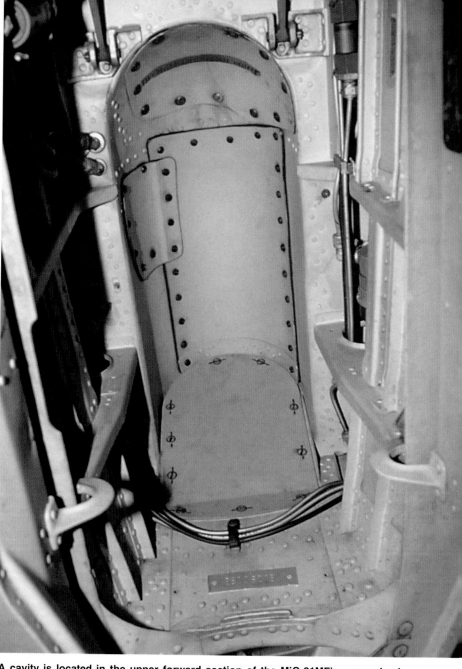

A cavity is located in the upper forward section of the MiG-21MF's nose wheel well. This cavity properly accommodated the KT-102 nose wheel. The nose gear doors are mounted to the lower fuselage with three sets of hinges, including the front set near the bay's forward end. Red lines painted on the forward bulkhead screw positions indicated fastened settings to mechanics.

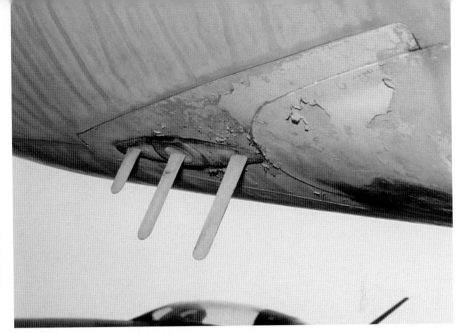

A disc brake pressurized air feed line ran down the nose landing gear strut's right side. This pipe ran from a reservoir in the forward fuselage down to the right rim of the KT-102 nose wheel. This MiG-21MF's nose wheel is placed on a plinth that reduced stress on the gear and tire.

The MiG-21MF's left nose wheel door was a mirror image of the right nose wheel door. Both Fishbed J nose gear doors were normally closed mechanically. A pneumatic (pressurized air) system was used in case of a main system failure. A hydraulic actuator mounted on the door pulled the door closed on gear retraction and extended the door open on gear extension.

The three-rod antenna for the SRO-2 *Khrom* (Chromium; NATO designation Odd Rods) Identification Friend or Foe (IFF) was mounted immediately ahead of the nose wheel well. The SRO-2 *Khrom* was used by all MiG-21 variants and on several other Soviet military aircraft and airliners, including the Tupolev Tu-134 (NATO code name Crusty) airliner.

Just above the left nose wheel door is the RP-22S *Sapfir* 21 radar (NATO designation Jay Bird) temperature probe, which only appeared on the left side. The temperature probe's location was adopted by late production MiG-21PFMs. Standard production MiG-21PFMs and all MiG-21Rs had the temperature probe mounted slightly behind the nose wheel well.

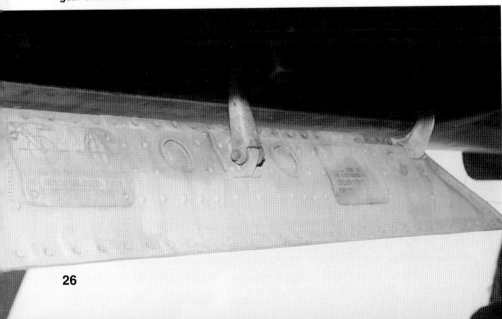

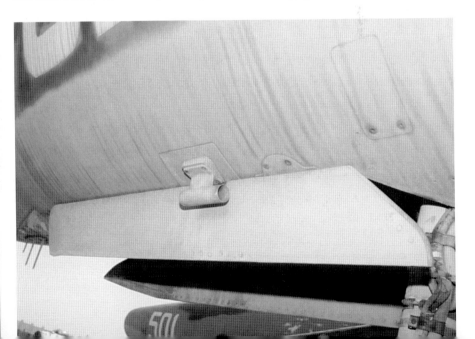

A small light is mounted on the upper area of the nose wheel strut's right side. This light indicated to the ground crew that the strut was properly extended for landing. Wiring for this light ran along the strut from a generator inside the well. The UP-53/1M valve for the anti-skid brake system was attached to the nose wheel strut's rear section. Compressed air passed from a fuselage reservoir through that valve into the brakes.

The MiG-21MF's nose wheel strut ran down from the aft section of the nose wheel well. A radar system temperature probe is located on the left side, just above the nose wheel doors. This probe fed air temperature data to the radar, which was mounted inside the nose cone.

(Above) The ejection seat and canopy jettison safety pins were installed on this *Polskie Wojska Lotnicze* (PWL; Polish Air Force) MiG-21 (Red 6506/Serial Number 966506). This was the most common situation when the Fishbed was parked on the ground. Metal rings protected several switches on the right console and sidewall. Ground crewmen preset most cockpit switches before a mission. (Marcus Fülber)

Third and Fourth Generation MiG-21s

VVS Designation	**OKB Designation**	**First Flight**	**NATO Name**
MiG-21S	Ye-7S, Type 95	1964	Fishbed J
MiG-21SM	Type 15	1967	Fishbed J
MiG-21M	Type 96	1968	Fishbed J
MiG-21MF	Type 96F	1970	Fishbed J
MiG-21bis *Lazur*/SAU	Type 7bis, Type 75	1971	Fishbed L/N

VVS: *Voenno Vozdushnye Sili* (Soviet Air Force)
OKB: *Opytnoe Konstrukctorskoe Byuro* (Experimental Design Bureau)
NATO: North Atlantic Treaty Organization

(Left) The same PWL MiG-21MF's tactical number (6506) is painted White on the ASP-PFD-21A gun sight assembly and the adjoining SSh-45-100OS gun camera. The circular RP-22S *Sapfir* 21 radar scope with its Black rubber viewing hood is offset just right of the panel's center. Several different interior colors were used on Fishbed Js. This MiG-21MF's cockpit is painted in Pale Peacock Blue (FS25299), which was a Blue-Green shade. Soviet researchers found this shade most soothing for pilots. (Marcus Fülber)

The ASP-PFD-21A gun sight is covered atop the instrument panel of this LSK NVA (East German Air Force) MiG-21MF (Red 513/Serial Number 8613). Flight instruments are mounted on the panel's left side, while the right contained engine, hydraulic, and fuel system gauges. A White stripe is painted down the panel's middle. (Harald Ziewe)

A radarscope is located in the MiG-21MF's lower right instrument panel section. This scope allowed the pilot to view returns from the nose-mounted RP-22S *Sapfir* 21 radar. A Red cover is fitted over the control stick grip. This prevents accidental systems actuation while the aircraft is on the ground. (Harald Ziewe)

This former LSK NVA MiG-21MF (Red 513/Serial Number 8613) differed in instrument panel details from *Polskie Wojska Lotnicze* (PWL; Polish Air Force) MiG-21MFs. The cockpit interior is painted a Light Green. Following German reunification in 1990, the *Bundesluftwaffe* (Federal German Air Force) tested this Fishbed J at Manching, Bavaria and assigned it the registration number 23+17. This number is painted on the Red control stick covering. (Harald Ziewe)

A *Letectvo Ceskoslovenske Lidove Armady* (LCLA; Czechoslovak People's Army Air Force) pilot performs the last pre-flight check with his mechanic. The pilot's White ZSh-3 helmet has a Blue-tinted visor. The overall natural metal MiG-21MF is parked in a shelter. The canopy support strut is attached on the upper windshield frame. This MiG-21MF has a White curtain in the aft canopy section; however, other Fishbed Js used a Dark Blue curtain and some MiG-21MFs had this curtain removed. The curtain kept excess light out of the cockpit during instrument flight conditions. (Zdenek Hurt)

The canopy support strut is attached on the upper windshield frame. This strut was painted in the same cockpit interior color, which was usually Pale Peacock Blue.

The canopy support strut connects the upper windshield frame and the right canopy side. This is used when the canopy was opened for prolonged periods and prevented a gust of wing from blowing the canopy closed. The strut is folded and stowed parallel to the left canopy frame.

The MiG-21MF's canopy was opened using this flush-mounted mechanism. This mechanism was located slightly below the windshield on the left cockpit side. The handle was pulled out and turned down to open the canopy. The reverse procedure closed and locked the canopy.

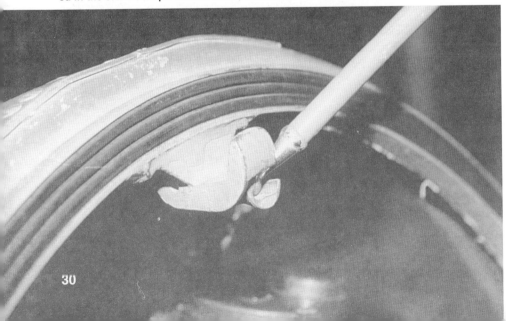

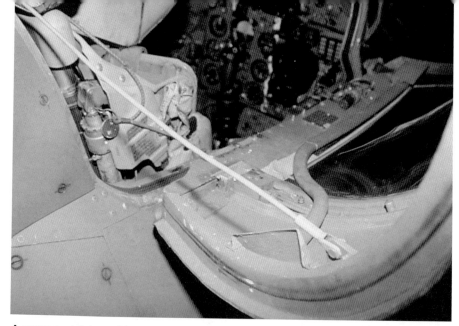

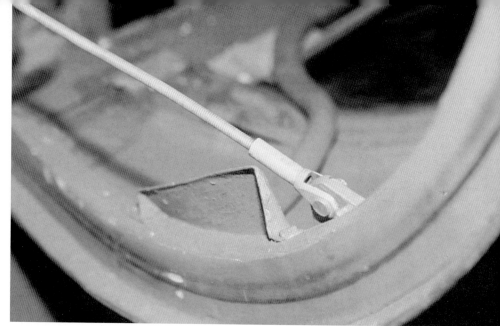

A canopy retaining cable was mounted to the aft canopy section. It connected the canopy and the rear cockpit area. This MiG-21MF had its aft canopy section curtain removed. This was done on several Fishbed Js in operational service.

A cable ran from the canopy sill in the cockpit to the front section of the MiG-21MF's right canopy closing mechanism. Electrical wires within this cable supplied power for the canopy locking mechanism. This mechanism insured the canopy's close fitting seal to the fuselage.

The canopy cable was attached to the rear canopy frame. This Silver cable – combined with the support strut in the front – kept the open canopy in position and prevented the canopy from over extending and damaging the hinges.

The canopy is open on this former East German MiG-21MF (Red 513/Serial Number 8613). This Fishbed J has a Dark Blue curtain located in the rear canopy section. The canopy support strut was folded and rests besides the left canopy framing. Electrical wiring for heating the rear view mirror run from the mirror assembly's front section to the canopy's front edge. (Harald Ziewe)

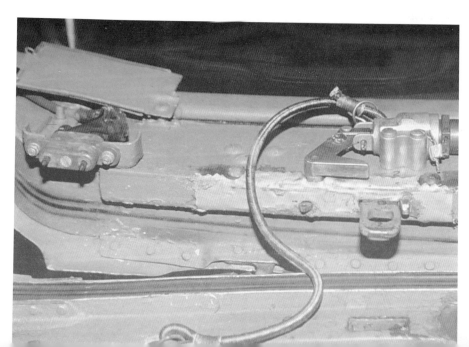

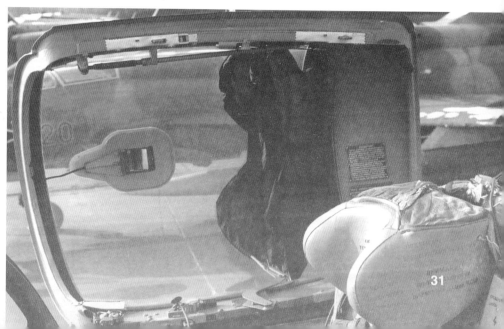

31

A Red emergency landing gear release button with White lettering is mounted on the right edge of the MiG-21MF's instrument panel. This button was painted Black on some MiG-21s. The radar scope with viewing hood is mounted on the panel across from the emergency landing gear release button.

A small circular pressure gauge is mounted on the aft end of the MiG-21MF's left cockpit wall. The ground crew pre-set the Red knobs protected by a plexiglass bar before a mission. These knobs were not used by the pilot during the flight. The throttle immediately beside the Red knobs is pulled fully aft.

Metal rings protect several switches mounted on the right cockpit console and wall. These rings prevented inadvertent actuation of these controls. Other switches were for the RP-22S *Sapfir* 21 radar and the ARK-10 radio compass. Brown knobs cover circuit breakers on the aft cockpit wall section.

Oxygen supply controls are mounted in the Silver box mounted atop the left cockpit console. The pilot used these to regulate the flow of oxygen for breathing at high altitude. Two Black oxygen hoses feed into the lower console wall just above the cockpit floor. These hoses were connected to the pilot's helmet.

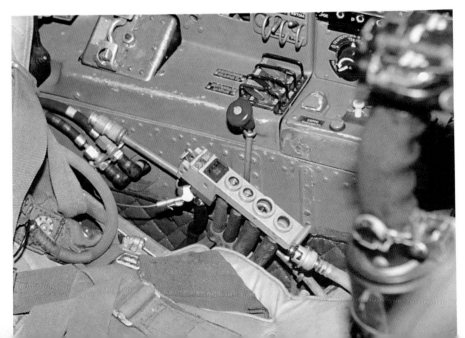

The throttle is located on the left console's front section. It was pushed forward to increase power and pulled aft to reduce power. A knob for the R-802 (RSIU-5V) communication radio was placed on the throttle control. Just in front of the throttle is the flap control panel. Oxygen hoses are held inside the Brown canvas sleeve secured to the cockpit wall. (Harald Ziewe)

Immediately aft of the throttle is the *Lazur* (Azure) Ground Control Intercept (GCI) system. Ground controllers guided pilots to their targets through radio messages, which were usually uncoded ('in the clear'). The Soviets and their clients usually employed GCI for MiG-21 pilots. This system did not allow pilots much flexibility in adjusting to tactical situation changes.

The MiG-21MF control stick is hinged in two bearing mounts. There are five push buttons and one switch on the control stick. The Black button on the right upper side turned off the AP-155 autopilot. The White target-tracking button is located under a Red button on the left side, while the gun-firing button is on the stick handle's rear upper side. A protective guard covers the fuselage external tank release button on the handle's lower section. The trim unit switch is located between the autopilot buttons.

The ASP-PFD-21A optical gun sight is mounted atop the MiG-21MF's instrument panel. An SSh-45-100OS gun camera is located to the sight's right. This camera recorded the results of actual and training combat for later study. Most SSh-45-100OS cameras were painted Black, but some were in Silver. The DVA-3A Angle of Attack (AoA) indicator is mounted above the gun camera.

The MiG-21MF and other Fishbed variants employed the same pair of rudder pedals. This right pedal shows the dimpled pedal surface, which allowed for easier grip by the pilot's boot. Leather straps on the inboard side kept the pilot's foot from easily slipping off the pedal. Paint rubbed off from the lower cockpit section due to wear over the fighter's service life.

A secondary panel was located just below the MiG-21MF's main instrument panel and just ahead of the control stick. The annunciator panel located to the right contained warning lights for various aircraft systems. Barometric instruments were placed on the secondary panel's lower section.

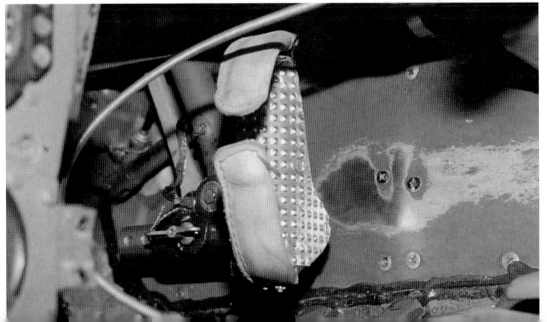

A TS-27AMSh rear view mirror was mounted atop the MiG-21MF's canopy. The pilot looked up into the angled mirror to see what was behind his aircraft. This same mirror was also installed on the later MiG-21*bis* (Fishbed L/N). Earlier MiG-21SM/Ms lacked the rear view mirror in the canopy, but some of these Fishbeds were retrofitted with the TS-27AMSh.

The TS-27AMSh rear view mirror's lower section is located just inside the canopy's upper section. Flush screws secured the lower section to the upper section that projected above the canopy surface. An electrical heating cable for this mirror led from the canopy frame into the TS-27AMSh. The heating system kept the mirror clear on cold days, when the mirror would otherwise fog up and obscure the pilot's rearward view.

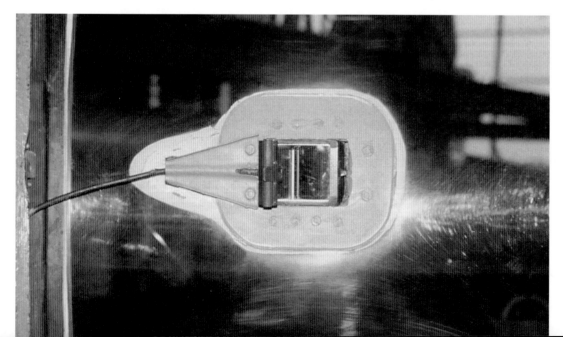

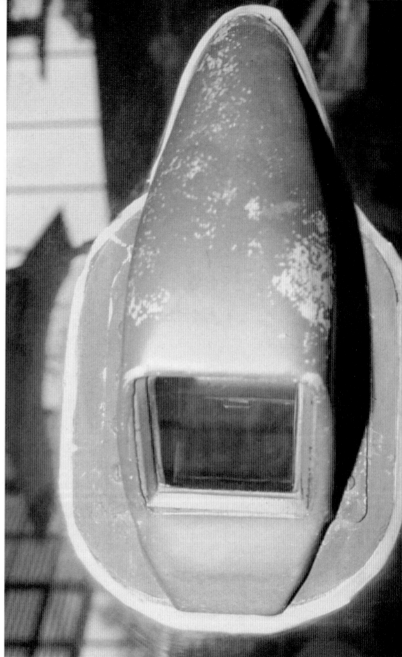

The TS-27AMSh rear view mirror was mounted in the canopies of third and fourth generation MiG-21s. This mirror provided a 35° rear view arc, but restricted upward visibility. MiG-21MF pilots had lower visibility than pilots of nearly all contemporary Western fighters.

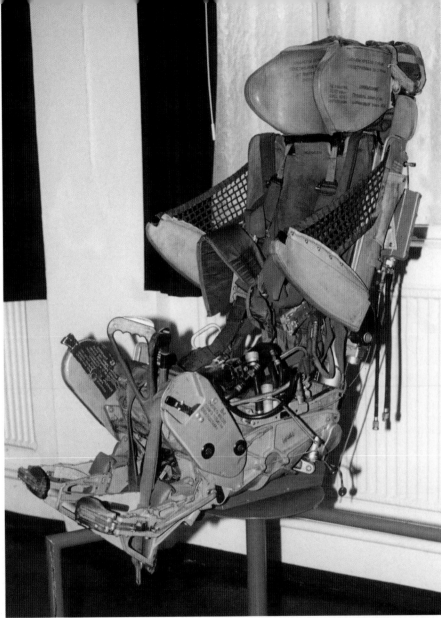

The KM-1M (*Kryeslo Mikoyana*; Mikoyan Seat) ejection seat was installed on all third and fourth generation MiG-21s. Upon ignition of the PZ-M solid rocket motor, communication and oxygen systems were disconnected. Simultaneously, the leg restraints were actuated and the stabilizing parachute deployed. The PS-M recovery chute was deployed once the pilot automatically separated from the seat. KM-1 seats were mostly painted Light Gray. A Red handle for ground egress or manual override situations was located in the right knee guard. The seat-pilot separation mechanism was integrated in the parachute pack. (Marcus Fülber)

The MiG-21MF's KM-1M ejection seat included a NAZ-7 survival kit packed into the seat cushion. This kit included three days' rations, a knife, waterproof matches, water disinfectant, and a survival radio. On the left knee guard is a Black inertia reel handle. It is pulled to activate the inertia reel, which is a belt that holds the pilot firmly in his seat for ejection. Folding support arms are located on both seat sides. The KM-1M allowed safe ejections at speeds from 130 KMH (81 MPH) to 1200 KMH (746 MPH) and at altitudes ranging from ground level to 25,000 M (82,021 feet). The pilot was automatically separated from the seat at a safe altitude through a timing mechanism inside the KM-1M. (Marcus Fülber)

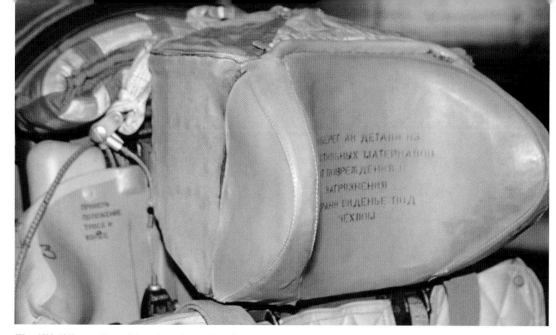

The KM-1M's scalloped headrest kept the pilot's head in the proper position for ejection. This East German MiG-21MF's headrest has a Black Cyrillic-lettered Russian inscription in the headrest's center, which did not appear on all KM-1M ejection seats. The rest's front face was made of leather, while the side and upper parts were made of fabric.

A 2 м² (21.5-square foot) extraction parachute is housed within the KM-1M headrest. Left of this headrest is the 0.1 м² (1.1-square foot) stabilizing parachute. This stabilizing parachute opened soon after ejection and steadled the pilot and seat prior to extraction parachute deployment. The Silver pipe mounted on the aft bulkhead beside the seat fed air from the air conditioning system into the cockpit. This provided for an optimal air temperature and pressure in all flight conditions.

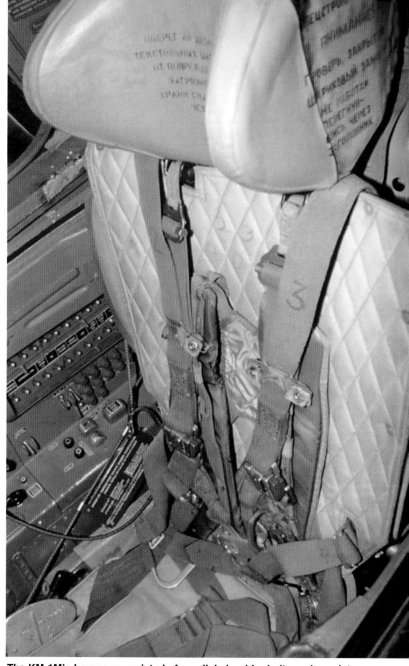

The KM-1M's harness consisted of parallel shoulder belts and a waist belt. These belts were made from Gray canvas. The harness was restrained upon ejection sequence activation. Harness restraining cylinders are located in the seat's right rear section, which is out of camera view.

The extraction parachute is packed inside the KM-1M's headrest, while the stabilizing parachute package is to the left and behind the headrest. The PZ-M solid rocket motor's upper section protrudes aft of the stabilizing parachute. The KM-1M produced a 20 g (20 times the amount of gravity) load on the pilot during ejection. (Harald Ziewe)

Part of the harness rests on the seat. The Red handle mounted on the right knee guard is for ground egress or manual override situations. Both main ejection handles were placed just in front of the control stick. Pulling up on these handles initiated the ejection sequence. These handles were pulled aft to arm the seat and pushed forward to disarm it.

The PZ-M solid rocket motor was mounted in the center of the KM-1M ejection seat's rear section. A PV-50 pyrotechnic cartridge mounted on the PZ-M's left side ignited the rocket motor. The box mounted on the far left contains the KPA-4 parachute opener. Tubes on the right are part of the harness tightening mechanism.

A Red ground egress or manual override situations handle is mounted on the right knee guard. This allowed the pilot to safely leave his seat due to a ground emergency or to prevent automatic seat separation during ejection. The upper part of the knee guard is painted Red, while the rest remained in Light Gray.

The KM-1M's two main ejection handles are mounted on the seat front at approximately 45° angles. These handles were either painted in Black or Brown. The pilot gripped these handles and pulled on them simultaneously to initiate the ejection sequence. The ejection handles flank the control stick, which is mounted to the cockpit floor.

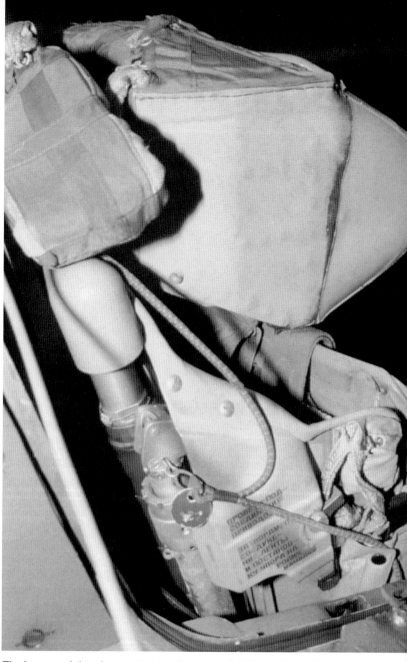

The harness tightening mechanism is housed within a tube behind the seat. This tube is mounted on the KM-1M's right rear section. Red safety pins were removed just prior to the mission, after the pilot was secured in his seat.

The position light is mounted on the outboard area of the MiG-21MF's wing leading edge. This light is Green on the right wing and Red on the left. A Radome Green dielectric panel covers the SOD-57M transponder near the position light. The White button-shaped antenna is for the SRZO-2 Identification Friend or Foe (IFF) system. A Red SPO-10 *Sirena* (Siren) Radar Homing And Warning (RHAW) antenna is located on the inboard wing leading edge.

White antennas for the SRZO-2 IFF system were also mounted on both wing leading edges on the MiG-21MF. IFF employs coded radio signals that are automatically sent to and received from the aircraft. These alert other aircraft and surface stations of the Fishbed's presence and warn the pilot of hostile aircraft in the vicinity.

SPO-10 *Sirena* RHAW antennas were mounted on both MiG-21MF wing leading edges. RHAW systems detected radars from other aircraft and surface stations that detected the MiG-21MF and warned the pilot of these emissions. The same button-shaped antennas were also mounted on the earlier MiG-21SM/M and the later MiG-21*bis*.

A Green position light is mounted on the MiG-21MF's right wing leading edge near the wingtip. The left wing has a Red position light. A PT-125T transformer inside the fuselage powered both lights' 36 Volt lamps.

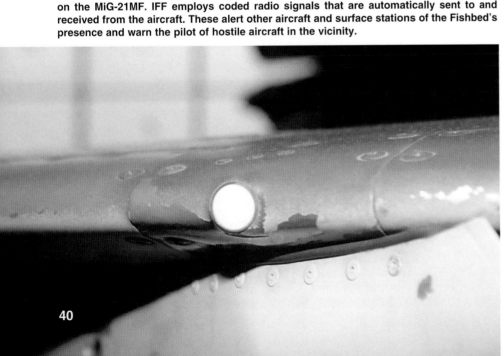

A static discharger is mounted on the rear of the MiG-21MF's left wingtip; another discharger is fitted to the right wingtip. Static electricity was dispersed through these dischargers. An airflow deflector bar mounted on the aileron's leading edge guided air over this surface. This resulted in greater aileron operational efficiency. All Fishbed variants had an upper surface wing fence on the left and right wings. This fence prevented spanwise airflow that interfered with transonic (Mach 0.8 to 1.2) flight.

Each MiG-21MF wing had a hydraulically operated flap located on its lower surface. This flap is set at 25° for take off and 45° for landing. MiG-21 flaps have all-metal surfaces and structure. Lowering the flap increased the wing's surface area at critical angles of attack, resulting in the aircraft maintaining lift at lower speeds.

One static discharger was mounted to each wingtip's rear surface. The static discharger remained unchanged on the third and fourth generation MiG-21s. Static electricity collected on the airframe through friction with the air was discharged through this item. This measure reduced the risk of short circuits in the aircraft's electrical system.

Flat-headed pins were located in recesses inboard and outboard of the flap inner surfaces. These pins secured the flap in the fully retracted position for level flight. MiG-21MF flaps employed low-wearing bust and bearing (pin and track) type hinges on both forward flap ends. These hinges used pins in the flaps that smoothly traveled through a track in the wing.

A wing fence was mounted on the MiG-21MF's left and right upper wing surfaces. The MiG-21SM/M employed the same wing fence design. This thin metal fence was bolted to the wing upper surface.

Aileron sway brace fairings were mounted on the MiG-21MF's upper and lower wing surfaces. The fairings provided streamlined coverage of the sway braces. BU-45A hydraulic boosters actuated these ailerons, whose deflection range was +/-20°.

MiG-21MFs had a retractable MPRF-1A landing light in each wing's undersurface immediately aft of the main wheel well. This front-hinged light extended while the aircraft taxied or was on final approach for landing. This former East German MiG-21MF (Red 687/Serial Number 6215) exhibited at the Schleissheim Aviation Museum has a lamp built by the American firm General Electric (GE).

A T-shaped dipole antenna for the RV-UM radio altimeter is mounted on both lower wingtip surfaces. The conical end pointed towards the front. Early MiG-21MFs had two triangle-shaped reinforcements on the horizontal boom's base. These reinforcements were mounted on most MiG-21MFs, but were deleted on later Fishbed Js.

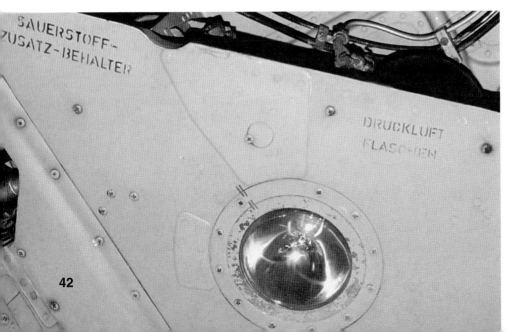

An APU-13MT missile rail is mounted on a MiG-21MF's left inboard BDZ-60-21D pylon. Two sets of sway braces prevented the rail from swinging laterally during flight. This rail carried the R-3S (NATO designation AA-2 Atoll) Infrared (IR) homing Air-to-Air Missile (AAM). APU-13MTs could be fitted to each of the Fishbed J's four wing pylons.

A 490 L (129-gallon) fuel tank is mounted on the left outboard pylon. This tank was secured to the pylon through a series of connectors. Fuel flowed out of the tank through the second connector from the front. MiG-21MFs could carry two fuel tanks on the outboard wing pylons and a third on the centerline pylon for increased range.

Several *Voenno Vozdushnye Sili* (VVS: Soviet Air Force) MiG-21MFs were converted for reconnaissance duties during the Soviet-Afghanistan War (1979-1988). A D-99 daylight reconnaissance pod replaced the centerline pylon. This pod housed one oblique camera in the nose and six vertical cameras further aft. A typical D-99 pod weighed 285 KG (628 pounds). This MiG-21MF (Black 35) carried 490 L fuel tanks on the outer pylons. The Fishbed J was assigned to the 263rd *Otdel'naya Razvedivatel'naya Aviatsiya Eskadril'ya* (ORAE: Detached Reconnaissance Aviation Squadron). This Squadron operated from Bagram Air Base approximately 47 KM (29 miles) north of the Afghan capital of Kabul during 1983. (Sergej F. Sergejev)

Maintenance crews gather on or in front of the same 263rd ORAE MiG-21MF (Black 35). A D-99 daylight reconnaissance pod is mounted on the centerline. The Black tactical number has a narrow White outline. Three Hero of the Soviet Union awards — Gold stars with Red ribbons — were painted as mission markings behind the tactical number. Reconnaissance-configured MiG-21s had a temperature probe mounted slightly aft of the nose wheel well, instead of above the nose wheel door on MiG-21MFs. This MiG-21MF flew from Bagram Air Base, Afghanistan during 1983. (Sergej F. Sergejev)

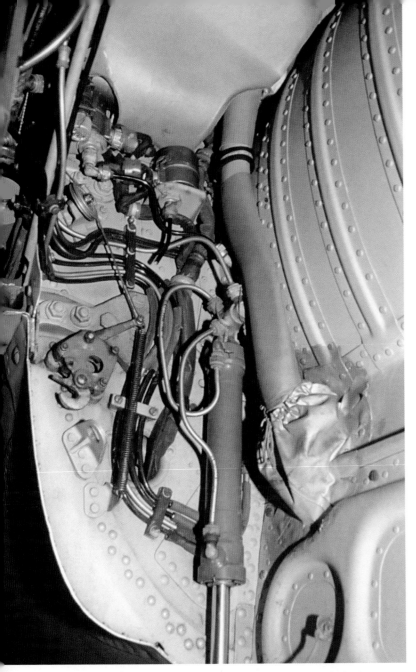

The right main wheel well was similar in configuration to that of the left main wheel well; however, the right well lacks the six square-shaped reinforcements found on the left well's lower section. The wheel well interior is painted a Light Green anti-corrosion paint, while the inner gear door surfaces are the same Pale Blue as the aircraft's undersurfaces.

The MiG-21MF's main wheel door was the same as on the earlier MiG-21SM/M. This door operated mechanically to completely enclose the main wheel on retraction. Left and right main wheel doors were identical. The main wheel doors were lowered or closed mechanically. The aircraft's serial number (6215) painted in Black stenciling on the door surface insured its return to the same airframe during major maintenance.

Several hydraulic pipes and electrical wires run through the front section of an East German MiG-21MF's left main wheel well. This Fishbed J's main wheel well is painted Light Gray. Other MiG-21MFs had this well painted the same Light Gray as the aircraft's undersurfaces.

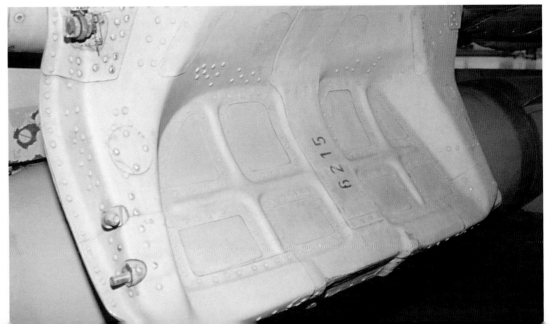

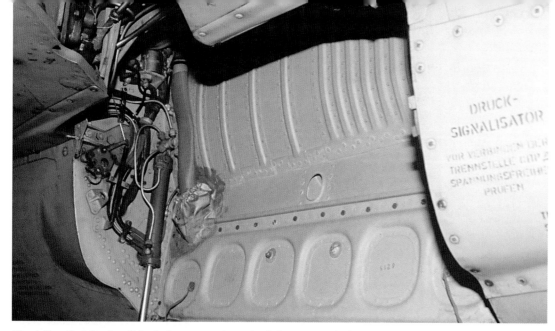

The left main wheel well had six square-shaped reinforcements in its lower section. These reinforcements were not found on the right main wheel well. Vertical stabilization ribs differed in layout between the left and right wells. The gear door actuating cylinder is mounted on the aft well bulkhead. This cylinder was connected to the door and raised it on gear retraction.

Yellow fuel pipes run down the fore and aft sections of the MiG-21MF's left main wheel well. Hydraulic pipe and electrical wiring arrangements differed in this well compared to those in the right main wheel well. Structural reinforcement ribs were mounted in the well's roof and side. This former LSK NVA (East German Air Force) MiG-21MF had Pale Blue gear wells and door inner surfaces.

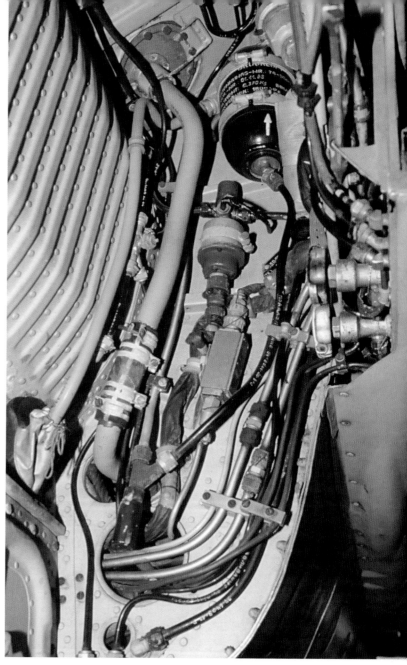

This is the aft section of a MiG-21MF's left main wheel well. The Yellow fuel pipe runs on the well's wall. This color was standard among Warsaw Pact air forces. Additional piping colors were Blue for oxygen and Black for pressurized air. Standardized piping colors aided ground crews, most of whom were conscripts.

45

The MiG-21MF employs KT-92B (*Koleso Tarmaznoye*; Braked Wheel) main wheels. This wheel rotated 87° around its axis during landing gear retraction. This allowed the wheel to rest vertically inside the well. Hydraulic actuators operated the landing gear, which also employed a pressurized air emergency extension system.

A two-part main wheel strut door is fitted outboard of the main wheel strut. The main landing gear legs are fitted with hydro-pneumatic shock absorbers. The tire fitted to the KT-92B is 800ᴍᴍ (31.5 inches) in diameter by 200ᴍᴍ (7.9 inches) wide. They were larger than the 660ᴍᴍ (26-inch) by 200ᴍᴍ tires fitted to first generation MiG-21s.

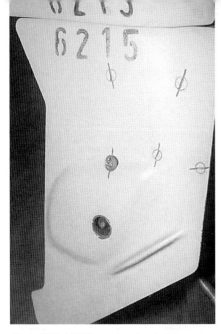

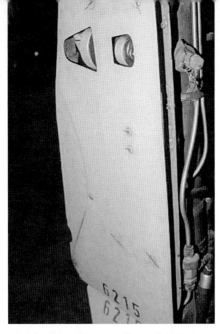

Each MiG-21MF's main wheel door came in two sections. The lower part jutted outboard of the strut and wheel. This aircraft's serial number (6215) is painted on both door parts.

The larger upper section of the main wheel door was mounted parallel to the main strut. Two small cutouts in the door allow for ground inspection of landing gear components.

A hydraulic actuator is mounted in the right wheel well's aft section. This actuator was connected to the main strut's inboard section. The actuator pulled up the main strut during landing gear retraction and lowered it on gear extension.

Inboard of the right KT-92B main wheel is the complex 'Parallellogram' mechanical linkage system. This rotated the main wheel 87° on retraction to keep this wheel upright in the well when the gear was fully retracted. A UA-24 anti-skid sensor is mounted on the right area of the wheel rim.

A KT-92B main wheel is mounted on the right gear strut of a *Bulgarski Voyenno Vozdushni Sili* (BVVS: Bulgarian Air Force) MiG-21MF. Disc brakes were fitted to the Fishbed J's main wheels. The KT-92B was also used on the previous MiG-21SM/M variants. Some KT-92Bs had the triangle-shaped depressions covered. Six triangular openings in the wheel vented cooling air to the brake assembly.

The Tumansky R-13-300 is a two-shaft axial flow turbojet engine with a modulated after-burner. This afterburner's fuel flow continuously varied to smoothly increase thrust. The engine's thrust ratings were 8973 pounds dry (non-afterburning) and 14,308 pounds in afterburner. The R-13-300 has a twin-section twin-shaft compressor with a three-stage section. The combustion chamber has ten annular (circular) combustion liners. A high-pressure shaft drives the auxiliary gearbox. Most of the auxiliary equipment was mounted below the engine. A low-pressure shaft drove the front oil pump. The starter-generator drives the engine by multiple-disc clutch and by ratchet or roller clutch. The R-13-300 has a total lifetime of 1500 hours with a Time Between Overhauls (TBO) of 500 hours. The R-13-300 weighs 1116 KG (2460 pounds). (Marcus Fülber)

A *Polskie Wojska Lotnicze* (PWL; Polish Air Force) MiG-21MF undergoes an overhaul. All access hatches were removed. Polish MiG-21MF airframe interiors were painted Chromate Green (approximately FS34552) as an anti-corrosion measure. The entire tail section was removed from the fuselage, which greatly eased access to the R-13-300 engine. (Marcus Fülber)

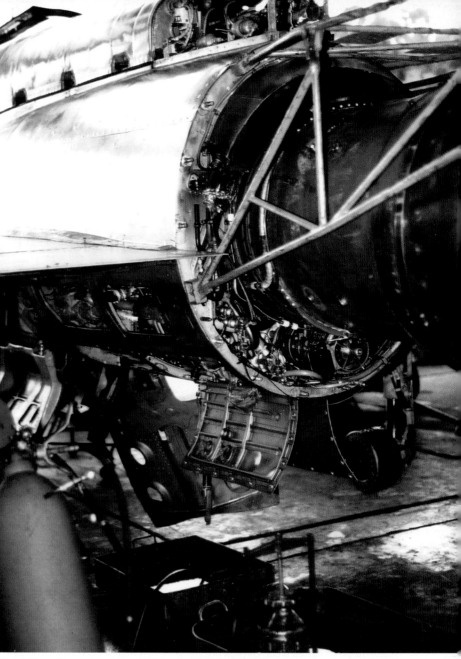

The tail section was removed from a PWL MiG-21MF during an overhaul. Blue spherical oxygen tanks were mounted within the Fishbed J's dorsal spine. Blue pipes ran from these tanks to the cockpit, where the pilot breathed the oxygen on high altitude flights.

The R-13-300's combustion chamber is exposed when the engine is pulled out of the aircraft for maintenance. Air from the engine's compressor is combined with fuel in this chamber, where it is ignited to produce energy. The combustion chamber is conical at its center. (Marcus Fülber)

Final stage turbine blades are seen through the rear of the R-13-300's convergent variable nozzle. Heated fuel-air mixture from the combustion chambers spun the turbine blades, which turned the engine shafts that spun the compressor blades. This heated gas then passed through the afterburner section and out of the engine as thrust.

The R-13-300's variable convergent nozzle has three hydraulic actuators located at the 2, 6, and 10 o'clock positions. This nozzle's opening expanded or contracted based upon engine power and flight conditions. The R-13-300 has an afterburner diameter of 900mm (35.7 inches). The nozzle temperature reaches 740° Celsius (1364° Fahrenheit) while the engine is at full power. (Harald Ziewe)

The MiG-21MF adopted the same easy engine maintenance system as the earlier Mikoyan-Gurevich MiG-15 (Fagot) and MiG-17 (Fresco) fighters. The entire tail section was removable from the aft fuselage. A special fixed steel tube boom was required to keep the R-13-300 engine in position during maintenance. This boom was mounted to the rear fuselage bulkhead when in use and removed from the aircraft after engine maintenance comple-

tion. The convergent variable nozzle optimizes the jet engine power output. The nozzle has a minimal diameter at maximum power without afterburner and from halfway to a fully open diameter with the afterburner on. The nozzle fully opens when the engine is idling. (Marcus Fülber)

Maintenance is performed on a *Polskie Wojska Lotnicze* (PWL; Polish Air Force) MiG-21MF. The aft speed brake was fully deployed and all rear fuselage access panels were removed. Removal of the aileron actuator fairing exposed this actuator on the lower wing surface. A main landing gear tire was removed from the KT-92B wheel. Warsaw Pact aircraft employed a color-coded piping system derived from that used on German jet aircraft late in World War Two. Hydraulic piping and units were either Gray or bare metal, pressurized air piping and units were Black, oxygen piping and tanks were Blue, the fuel system was Yellow, and the fire extinguishing system was Red. (Marcus Fülber)

Various access panels are removed from the left rear fuselage of a PWL MiG-21MF. The aft speed brake was disconnected from its actuating cylinder. This allowed the brake to fully extend from the lower fuselage, while the actuator rests vertically from its pivot point on the aircraft. The aileron actuator fairing was removed from the left wing undersurface.

Yellow fuel pipes run through the aft fuselage. These carried fuel from the fuel tanks in the mid-fuselage – or from the external fuel tanks – to the engine. A pan lies on the hangar floor below the aft fuselage. It is used to collect any fuel or other liquids leaking from the MiG-21MF during maintenance. (Marcus Fülber)

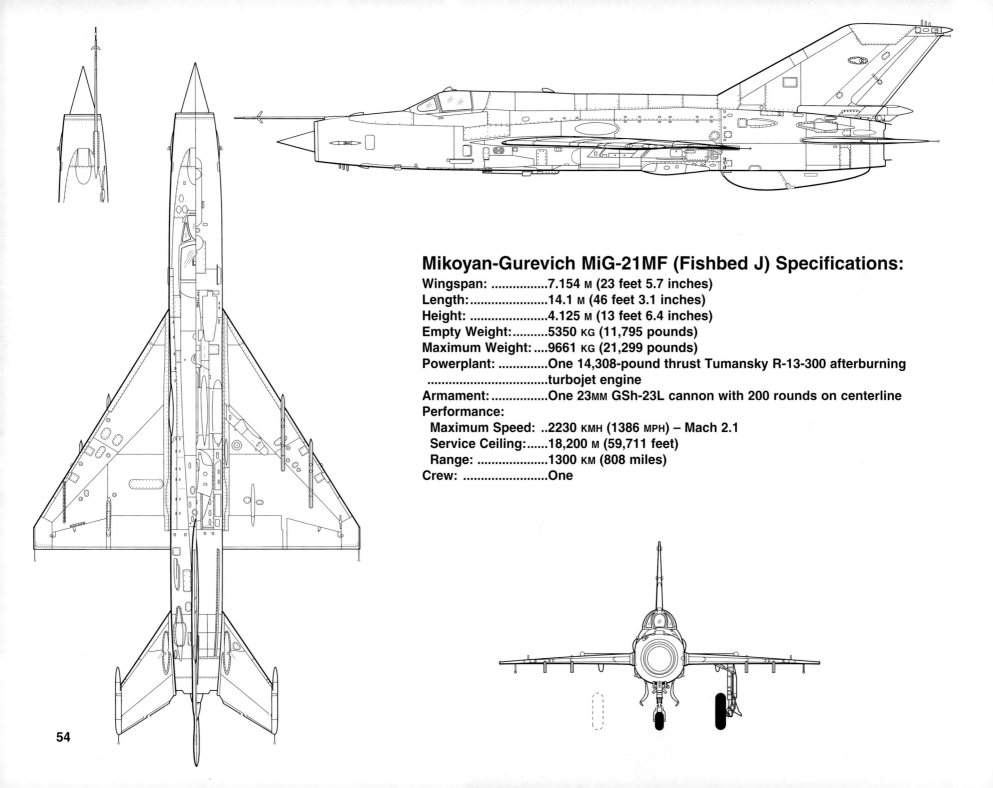

Mikoyan-Gurevich MiG-21MF (Fishbed J) Specifications:

Wingspan: ....7.154 м (23 feet 5.7 inches)
Length: ....14.1 м (46 feet 3.1 inches)
Height: ....4.125 м (13 feet 6.4 inches)
Empty Weight: ....5350 кг (11,795 pounds)
Maximum Weight: ....9661 кг (21,299 pounds)
Powerplant: ....One 14,308-pound thrust Tumansky R-13-300 afterburning
...............................turbojet engine
Armament: ....One 23мм GSh-23L cannon with 200 rounds on centerline
Performance:
  Maximum Speed: ..2230 кмн (1386 мрн) – Mach 2.1
  Service Ceiling: ......18,200 м (59,711 feet)
  Range: ....1300 км (808 miles)
Crew: ....One

Access panels were removed from this PWL (Polish Air Force) MiG-21MF. The left bay houses the SPO-10 Sirena Radar Homing and Warning (RHAW) system and the sight computing unit for the ASP-PFD-21A gun sight. Several small openings were cut into the fuselage auxiliary air inlet cover's surface. The insignia on the fuselage is for an unknown unit of the 3. *Korpus Lotniczy* (KL; Air Corps). (Marcus Fülber)

The external power hook up was mounted slightly below the left wing leading edge. The forward (left) socket is for 27 Volt, while the aft (right) socket is for the 115 Volt Auxiliary Power Unit (APU). The APU powered aircraft systems when the engine was not running.

A Polish pilot climbs into his overall natural metal MiG-21MF. Gun gas deflector plates – one each to left and right – were first mounted on this variant. Earlier Fishbeds lacked these plates. The deflector plates became necessary due to the centerline 23mm GSh-23L cannon. A muzzle blast from the weapon could blow upon the nearby auxiliary engine inlets when the aircraft was at a high angle of attack and low airspeed. This could result in a violent compressor stall. External power sockets are located under the left wing leading edge. The battery housing in front of the GSh-23L was partially opened for final pre-flight checks. (Andrzej Morgala)

Letectvo Ceskoslovenske Armady (LCA; Czechoslovak Army Air Force) mechanics service the KT-102 (*Koleso Tarmaznoye*; Braked Wheel) nose wheel of this MiG-21MF (Black 5302/Serial Number 965302). They jacked up the nose section in order to properly perform the maintenance. A cockpit access ladder is parked near the aircraft and a tarpaulin is folded on the left wing. (Sign via Roman Sekyrka)

The circular ARK-10 ADF covering was mounted on the lower fuselage. ADF is a navigational aid that employs radio signals sent from ground stations. Two metal fore-and-aft coils inside this panel tuned to these signals and sent course data to the cockpit. This cover is located between the main wheel well and the battery accumulator container. This covering was painted Radome Green (FS24108) on all MiG-21MFs. The East Germans did not change the Cyrillic letters APK to ARK when translating the Russian service stenciling to German on this MiG-21MF.

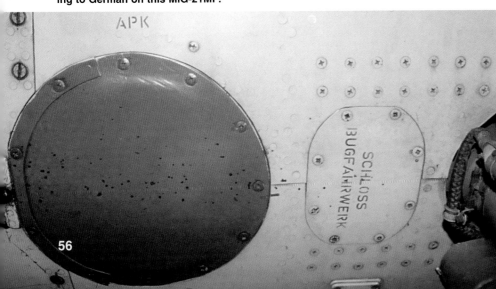

Two 15-SCS-45 accumulator batteries were housed in a container just behind the nose wheel strut. These batteries were charged by external power before flight and powered the aircraft's electrical systems during flight. The ARK-10 Automatic Direction Finder (ADF) covering is located in front of the battery housing. (Marcus Fülber)

MiG-21MFs employed two different types of fuselage auxiliary air inlet cover plates. The most popular plate had apertures fitted on its surface. The other cover plate was solid with an X-shaped fairing. These covers were painted Red for high visibility. A gun gas deflector plate is bolted immediately under this inlet.

Five cooling air slots are fitted in the AP-155 autopilot's right access panel. There are no slots on the left access panel. The autopilot access panel is located immediately aft of the cockpit section. MiG-21PF through MiG-21PFM variants had these slots on the left access panel, but not on the right.

SPRD-99 rocket attachment points are mounted on both MiG-21MF rear fuselage sides. Two SPRD-99s – one each to left and right – were mounted for Rocket Assisted Take-Off (RATO), which reduced the MiG-21MF's take-off distance. Both rockets ignited on the ground shortly after the afterburner was engaged.

The front SPRD-99 attachment point was located on fuselage frame 22. The rocket was released from the MiG-21MF's rear fuselage after take off. The SPRD-99 could only be used once and was usually destroyed when the equipment hit the ground. Those SPRD-99s that were recovered intact were returned to their manufacturer for refurbishment.

The rear SPRD-99 attachment point was mounted to frame 28 on the MiG-21MF's aft fuselage. These attachments were carried on both rear fuselage sides. Pressurized air aided in releasing the SPRD-99 from the aircraft after take off. RATO was introduced on the Fishbed family on the earlier MiG-21PFM (Fishbed F).

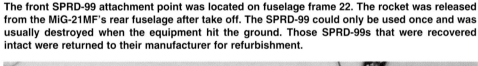

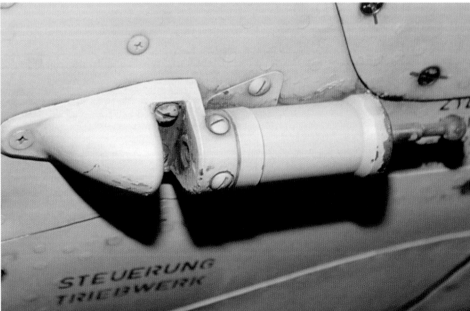

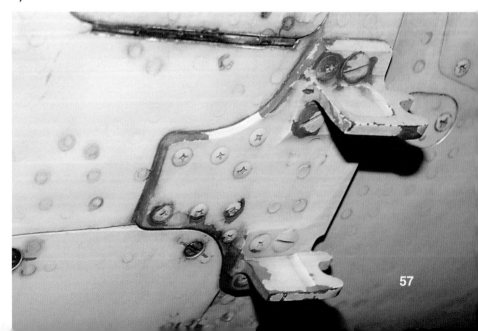

A ground crew refuels an overall natural metal *Polskie Wojska Lotnicze* (PWL; Polish Air Force) MiG-21MF (Red 8910/Serial Number 968910). Fuselage and wing tanks were refueled through a central point located just behind the cockpit section in the dorsal spine. The truck on the left sprays water for cleaning the runway. (Andrzej Morgala)

The central refueling point was located just in front of the air intake. Air passed through this intake pressurized the six fuselage fuel tanks. This allows for efficient fuel movement from the tanks through the fuel pipes to the engine.

This air intake mounted on the dorsal spine fed pressurized air to the six fuselage tanks. The intake was introduced on the MiG-21SM/M aircraft. Earlier MiG-21 variants lacked this inlet. The circular base plate was removed for servicing the fuel tank pressurization equipment.

The MiG-21MF's central refuelling point is located on the dorsal spine. It was opened using the flush-mounted latch within the circular cover. Single-point refueling helps reduce turnaround time between missions. The Fishbed J's total internal fuel capacity is 2600 L (687 gallons). This capacity was supplemented by up to three 490 L (129-gallon) external fuel tanks: One on the centerline pylon and two on the outboard wing pylons.

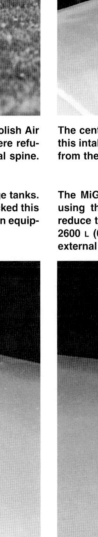

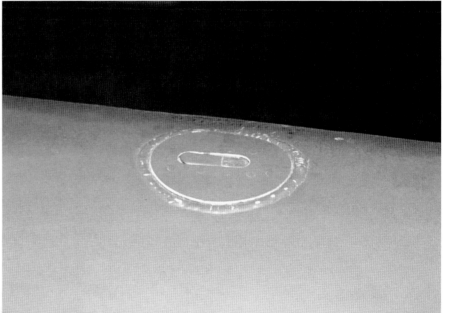

An SOD-57M Air Traffic Control (ATC) transponder antenna is located inside the MiG-21MF's tail tip cone. This broadcast the aircraft's signal to ground controllers. A static discharger is placed below the SOD-57M cone, with a White position light between the cone and the discharger.

Part of the dielectric panel covering the R-802 radio antenna is on the leading edge of the MiG-21MF's tailfin tip. An SRO-2 *Khrom* (Chromium; NATO designation Odd Rods) Identification Friend or Foe (IFF) system tripole antenna is mounted atop the fin. Aft-facing button-shaped antennas for the SPO-10 *Sirena* (Siren) Radar Homing And Warning (RHAW) system are fitted above the rudder. RHAW detects the presence of enemy airborne and surface radars, then sends a warning signal to the pilot.

A Polish ground crew maintains an overall natural metal MiG-21MF (Red 9114/Serial Number 969114) in October of 1974. The T-shaped RV-UM radio altimeter antenna lacks the triangle-shaped extension to the horizontal tube's upper section. This extension was found on most MiG-21MFs. The Radome Green dielectric panel on the upper tailfin covers the R-802 radio antenna. A small fairing above the Red and White Polish national insignia houses the KSI-2 compass' ID-2 induction sensor. This device read the earth's magnetic field to aid in determining the aircraft's position. A button-shaped antenna for the SPO-10 *Sirena* RHAW system is placed on the fairing's rear area. This fairing is located on both tailfin sides. (Andrzej Morgala)

59

The nozzle actuator cooling inlet is mounted on the aft fuselage, just above the longer nozzle hydraulic line fairing. The afterburner cooling inlet is mounted ahead of this fairing. A small inlet on the rear ventral fin fed additional cooling air into the nozzle actuator. These inlets are also located on the MiG-21MF's left rear fuselage. (Harald Ziewe)

The MiG-21MF's upper nozzle actuator cooling inlet is located above the fairing covering the nozzle hydraulic actuator. This fairing is fixed with screws on the skinning and is removable for maintenance purposes.

Nozzle hydraulic actuator lines run under the long, narrow fairing just above the MiG-21MF's stabilator (horizontal stabilizer/elevator). A Red rudder lock pin is installed on the PT-21UK brake parachute container's base. This pin kept the rudder from freely swinging when the Fishbed J was on the ground. Rudder travel range was 25° each to left and right, while the stabilators moved from +7° to -16.5°. (Harald Ziewe)

A large inlet was placed in front of the nozzle hydraulic actuator fairing. This intake fed cooling air into the afterburner section. Aft fuselage front and rear inlets differed in both size and layout. This inlet is on a Bulgarian MiG-21MF, but the earlier MiG-21SM/Ms used the same inlet types.

Maintenance is performed on a PWL (Polish Air Force) MiG-21MF. Part of the R-13-300 engine's nozzle was removed, along with the rear dorsal spine panel. These parts were attached to the aircraft using flush-mounted screws. Soviet and Warsaw Pact (WARPAC) doctrine called for combat units to perform basic maintenance at their bases, with scheduled overhauls performed at maintenance depots. (Marcus Fülber)

The triangle-shaped panel is removed from the left tailfin side of this PWL MiG-21MF. This tail section is removed from the fuselage during an overhaul. The structure and panel inner surfaces were painted Chromate Green as an anti-corrosion measure. The Orange box is the SARPP flight recorder used to store aircraft data for later evaluation. The Black NP-27T emergency hydraulic pump is located below the flight recorder. (Marcus Fülber)

Warsaw Pact Member States
1955 – 1991

Albania (withdrew 1968)
Bulgaria
Czechoslovakia
East Germany
Hungary
Poland
Romania
Soviet Union

The removed dorsal spine rear access panel reveals the Yellow fuel pipes, fuel pumps, and the GA-135T autopilot unit. Small rectangular access panels were used in disconnecting the tail from the rear fuselage. (Marcus Fülber)

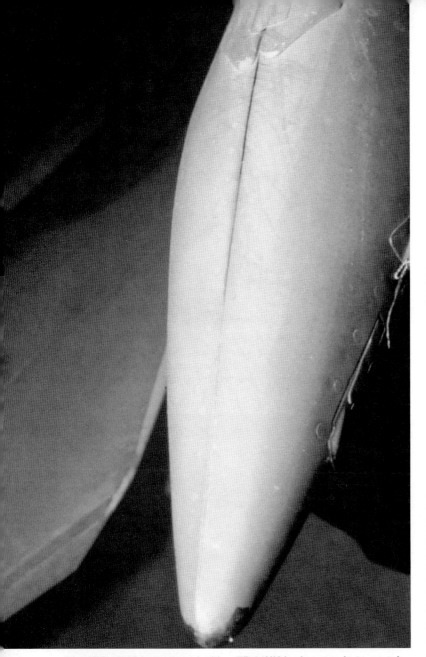

Stabsfeldwebel (Staff Sergeant) Klaus Jäckel inserts a brake parachute into an East German MiG-21MF's PT-21UK container. He stands on a cockpit access ladder to reach the parachute container. This occurred during an exercise held in September of 1981. MiG-21MFs employed either circular or cruciform (cross shaped) brake parachutes. (Hans-Joachim Mau)

The TP-21UK brake parachute container is located just above the engine nozzle. Two clamshell doors opened before the parachute deployed. This chute was deployed at landing speeds up to 320 кмн (199 мрн). The brake parachute fully opened 1.5 seconds after deploying. This slowed the aircraft's speed, which reduced the landing run and reduced wear on the brakes.

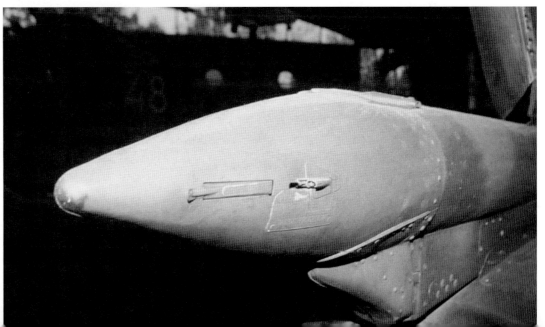

The MiG-21MF is equipped with a TP-21UK brake parachute container, which was located immediately below the rudder. A 16 м² (172.2-square foot) parachute was installed inside this container. The MiG-21PFM was the first Fishbed variant with the brake parachute container below the rudder. Early MiG-21s had the parachute installed in the left rear fuselage.

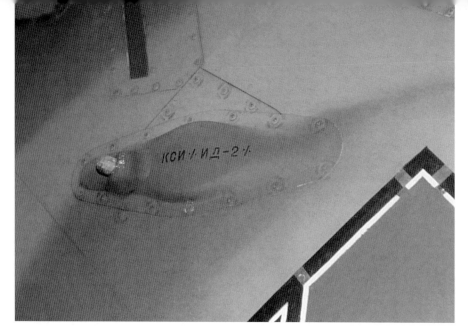

The KSI-2 compass' ID-2 induction sensor is fitting within a fairing on both MiG-21MF tail-fin sides. An SPO-10 *Sirena* RHAW system antenna is mounted on the fairing's left side. The earlier MiG-21PFM lacked the SPO-10's button-shaped antennas.

A thin metal sheet was mounted above the nozzle. This sheet protected the PT-21UK brake parachute from hot exhaust gases, which would otherwise damage the parachute canopy and lines.

The nozzle's lower cooling inlet is located on the ventral fin's upper rear section. One inlet was located on each ventral fin side. Both inlets fed cooling air to the engine nozzle. The ventral fin aided in providing stability in all flight regimes and was standard on all MiG-21 variants.

A fuel dump pipe was mounted only on the right nozzle side. The MiG-21MF's pilot used this pipe to dump excess fuel for lightening the aircraft. This procedure was done only in an emergency, such as for a 'wheels up' landing when the landing gear could not be extended.

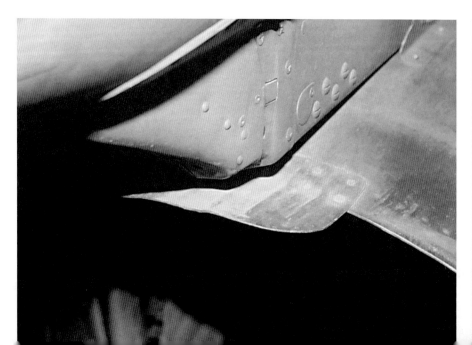

The *Letectvo Armady Ceske* (LAC; Czech Army Air Force) modified ten MiG-21MFs to RNAV (also called MiG-21MFN) standard. This modification made these aircraft compatible with North Atlantic Treaty Organization (NATO) standards. LOK Kbely performed the MiG-21MF/RNAV conversions at Caslav Air Base, Czech Republic. Antennas for the Raytheon AN/APX-100 IFF Mode 2 transponder are mounted behind the nose wheel bay and in front of the windshield. This overall Light Gray MiG-21MF/RNAV (Black 5581/Serial Number 96005581) of the 211th Tactical Flight, 21. *Základna Taktického Letectva* (ZTL; Tactical Air Base) taxies at Caslav Air Base on 23 May 2001. Black and Yellow tiger stripes are painted on the wing fences. (Jaroslav Farkas via JaPo Collection)

A small rectangular panel covers the aperture left by removing the T-shaped RV-UM radio altimeter antenna from the MiG-21MF/RNAV's lower wingtips. The new RV-5M radio altimeter replaced the RV-UM during the RNAV modification. Each RV-5M antenna was mounted in fairings located in front of and behind the main wheel bays. (Jaroslav Farkas via JaPo Collection)

An AN/APX-100 IFF antenna is mounted left of the PVD-7 air data boom atop the MiG-21MF/RNAV's nose. The AN/APX-100 replaced the American-made King KXP-756 Air Traffic Control (ATC) transponder originally retrofitted to Czech MiG-21MFs. The tripole SRO-2 *Khrom* (NATO designation Odd Rods) IFF antenna was deleted from the lower nose section. A blade antenna for the Rockwell Collins DME-42 Distance Measuring Equipment (DME) replaced the SRO-2 antenna. The Ramenskoye RV-5M radio altimeter antenna is in the fairing in front of the nose wheel bay. A German-made Hella Red anti-collision light is mounted aft and right of the nose wheel bay. (Jaroslav Farkas via JaPo Collection)

The MiG-21MF/RNAV deleted the SRO-2 *Khrom* triple rod IFF antenna atop the tailfin. This variant retained the R-802 radio within the upper tailfin dielectric panel. The Black antenna below this panel is for the Rockwell Collins VIR-32 radio navigation receiver. A Red anti-collision light is mounted immediately aft of the dorsal Trimble 2001 I/O Plus Ground Positioning System (GPS) blade antenna. A Levis sticker was attached to the aft ventral fin section. Low visibility 'tiger stripes' are painted on this aircraft's aft fuselage and tail. (Jaroslav Farkas via JaPo Collection)

The MiG-21*bis Lazur* (Azure) (Fishbed L) was externally similar to the earlier MiG-21MF; however, the new variant had a wider and deeper dorsal spine. This spine was faired further back into the vertical tail than on the MiG-21MF. Early MiG-21*bis Lazurs* were delivered in overall natural metal to the *Voenno Vozdushnye Sili* (VVS: Soviet Air Force). This aircraft (Blue 39/Serial Number 75012374) belonged to a VVS detachment that paid a courtesy visit to Kuopio-Rissala Air Base, Finland on 5-9 August 1974. There is a thin Black outline to the Blue tactical number. A 490 ʟ (129-gallon) fuel tank is mounted on each outer wing pylon. (Klaus Niska)

The MiG-21*bis* SAU (Fishbed N) featured the RSBN-2S (NATO designation Swift Rod) Instrument Landing System (ILS) antenna on the lower nose. This antenna was not mounted on previous Fishbed variants. Installation of the RSBN-2S antenna resulted in the SRO-2 *Khrom* IFF antenna being slightly offset to left. (Harald Ziewe)

The MiG-21*bis Lazur*'s nose section was nearly identical to the MiG-21MF. Most Fishbed Ls carried the SRO-2 *Khrom* IFF system triple pole antenna, but some aircraft were retrofitted with a blade-shaped IFF antenna. This MiG-21*bis Lazur* (Blue 40/Serial Number 75012400) also belonged to the Soviet contingent that visited Kuopio-Rissala Air Base in 1974. The Light Gray lower nose finish was non-standard on natural metal MiG-21*bis Lazurs*. *XVII S'YeED VAKSM* (17th Congress of Komsomol) is painted immediately aft of the tactical number. *Komsomol* (Young Communist League) was the All-Union Leninist Organization for 18- to 28-year old Soviet people. (Klaus Niska)

Several MiG-21*bis* aircraft were equipped with a blade-shaped IFF antenna instead of the standard three-pole antenna. This antenna was mounted slightly left of center on the MiG-21*bis* SAU's lower nose, due to the RSBN-2S ILS antenna's installation on the centerline. Late production MiG-21*bis Lazurs* also had the SRO-2's three-pole antenna offset to left, although the RSBN-2S was never mounted on the Fishbed L. (Stephan Boshniakov)

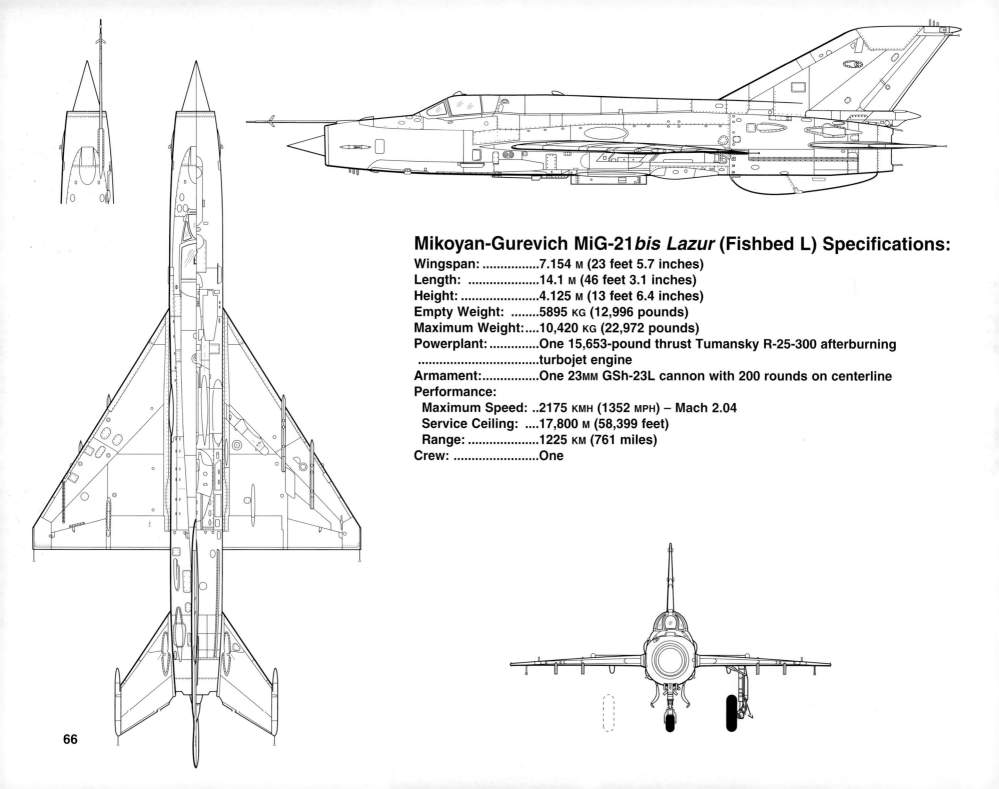

Mikoyan-Gurevich MiG-21*bis Lazur* (Fishbed L) Specifications:

Wingspan: ....7.154 м (23 feet 5.7 inches)
Length: ....14.1 м (46 feet 3.1 inches)
Height: ....4.125 м (13 feet 6.4 inches)
Empty Weight: ....5895 кG (12,996 pounds)
Maximum Weight:....10,420 кG (22,972 pounds)
Powerplant: ....One 15,653-pound thrust Tumansky R-25-300 afterburning
..................................turbojet engine
Armament:...............One 23мм GSh-23L cannon with 200 rounds on centerline
Performance:
  Maximum Speed: ..2175 кмн (1352 мрн) – Mach 2.04
  Service Ceiling: ....17,800 м (58,399 feet)
  Range: ....1225 км (761 miles)
Crew: ....One

The *Bulgarski Voyenno Vozdushni Sili* (BVVS: Bulgarian Air Force) flew this MiG-21*bis Lazur* (White 91/Serial Number 75080645). It was assigned to the 6. *Iztrebitelen Aviazionen Polk* (IAP; Fighter Aviation Regiment) at Balchik. The 6. IAP insignia is painted on the aircraft's nose. This former VVS (Soviet Air Force) MiG-21*bis Lazur* was transferred to the BVVS in 1990. Two R-60M (NATO designation AA-8 Aphid) Air-to-Air Missiles (AAMs) are mounted on an L-shaped APU-60-IIM double launcher attached to the outboard pylon. An APU-13 MT missile rail on the inboard wing pylon carries an R-3S (NATO designation AA-2 Atoll) AAM with an Infrared (IR) seeker. A blade-shaped IFF antenna replaced the SRO-2 *Khrom*'s original tripole antenna. The Communist-era Bulgarian national insignia on this aircraft was used between 1948 and 1992. (Stephan Boshniakov)

This MiG-21*bis Lazur* (White 85/Serial Number 75054147) has a uniquely Bulgarian SRO-2 IFF antenna modification. A Red blade-style antenna was mounted offset to the left, while a tripole antenna was located atop the left fuselage side. Both antennas worked with the SRO-2 *Khrom* system. The 6. IAP insignia is painted on the nose immediately forward of the tactical number. This former VVS MiG-21*bis Lazur* was allocated to the BVVS in 1990. (Stephan Boshniakov)

An additional tripole antenna was mounted atop the left fuselage of this Bulgarian MiG-21*bis Lazur* (White 501/Serial Number 75019901). This Fishbed N is now preserved at the Military Academy at Sofia, Bulgaria. It was yet another former Soviet MiG-21*bis Lazur* that was delivered to Bulgaria in 1990. (Stephan Boshniakov)

A position light is mounted on the right side of the MiG-21*bis Lazur*'s nose wheel strut. This light indicated to the ground crew that the nose wheel was properly deployed. Brake pneumatic gauge locations on the nose wheel strut differed from those on the earlier MiG-21MF (Fishbed J). The nosewheel of this retired BVVS aircraft is propped up on a plinth. (Stephan Boshniakov)

67

This cockpit belongs to a former LSK NVA (East German Air Force) MiG-21*bis* SAU (Red 846/Serial Number 75051402). The cockpit had several minor equipment and instrument changes from the MiG-21MF. The Angle of Attack (AoA) indicator was moved from a position above the SSh-45-100OS gun camera to the upper right instrument panel. A Black panel of knobs is located above the radarscope. This panel replaced switches that were above the MiG-21MF's radar scope. A switch believed to turn the gun camera on or off was added to the right side of the SSh-45-100OS. The MiG-21MF's gun sight did not have this switch. (Harald Ziewe)

The MiG-21*bis* SAU right console's front section layout was changed from that of the earlier MiG-21MF. This cockpit is on the same ex-East German MiG-21*bis* SAU (Red 846/Serial Number 75051402). A White vertical stripe is painted on the instrument panel's center area. Soviet-style pilots were taught to use this stripe as a visual cue for centering the control stick in the event of aircraft control difficulties. (Harald Ziewe)

The MiG-21*bis* SAU's right console was similar to that of a MiG-21MF, but several switches were changed on the later variant. The right console included instruments and switches for the RP-22SMA *Sapfir* (Sapphire) radar and the ARK-10 radio compass. The right-hinged cockpit canopy is opened on this Fishbed N. (Harald Ziewe)

The MiG-21*bis* SAU's left console was nearly identical to the one on the MiG-21MF. A rectangular Black panel is mounted on the cockpit wall. This panel replaced the two rows of Red switches covered by a clear plexiglass bar on the earlier MiG-21MF. Both the control stick grip and the windshield frame obscure the throttle quadrant on the console's forward section. (Harald Ziewe)

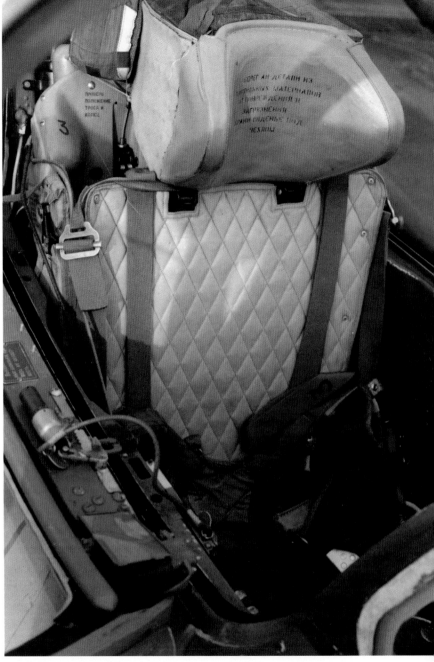

All MiG-21*bis* aircraft retained the well-proven KM-1M ejection seat from the MiG-21MF. KM-1Ms were the same for these variants, which allowed for their interchangability among third and fourth generation Fishbeds. (Harald Ziewe)

This MiG-21*bis Lazur* (White 91/Serial Number 75080645) was assigned to the 6. IAP (Fighter Aviation Regiment), BVVS (Bulgarian Air Force) at Balchik, Bulgaria. A temperature probe is mounted immediately beside the PVD-7 air data boom. This probe is unique to Bulgaria's and Croatia's MiG-21*bis* fighters (Stephan Boshniakov)

Maintenance is performed on a BVVS MiG-21*bis* SAU (White 243/Serial Number 75094243). It was delivered from the factory to the 19th IAP at Graf Ignatievo, near Plovdiv, in 1983. Late production MiG-21*bis Lazurs* and early MiG-21*bis* SAUs had the tripole 'Odd Rods' antenna installed on the lower left fuselage. This antenna was on the centerline on MiG-21MFs and early MiG-21*bis Lazurs*. The RP-22SMA *Sapfir* radar was removed to expose the rails on which the AV-711 actuator hydraulically moved the radar forward and aft. MiG-21*bis* variants had rectangular cooling inlets in the circular intake lip. These inlets were circular on earlier MiG-21M/MF. (Stephan Boshniakov)

Several *Ilmavoimat* (Finnish Air Force) MiG-21*bis Lazurs* are lined up. These aircraft were assigned to *Hävittäjälentolaivue* (HävLLv; Fighter Squadron) 31 at Kuopio-Rissala Air Base. The MiG-21*bis Lazurs* replaced older MiG-21F-12 (Fishbed C) aircraft in HävLLv 31. A plastic covering protects sensors on the PVD-7 air data boom. (Klaus Niska)

The MiG-21*bis'* deeper and wider spine is the Fishbed L/N's main external feature, compared to the MiG-21MF's more tapered spine. Enlarging the spine increased the MiG-21*bis'* internal fuel capacity to 2880 L (761 gallons). This was a 280 L (74-gallon) increase over the MiG-21MF's 2600 L (687-gallon) internal fuel capacity. (Harald Ziewe)

This BVVS MiG-21*bis Lazur* displays the new Bulgarian national markings that were introduced in 1992. The fighter is armed with two R-60M (AA-8 Aphid) Air-to-Air Missiles (AAMs) that are loaded onto an L-shaped APU-60-IIM double launcher on the outboard pylon. The R-60M is 1195mm (47 inches) long, 120mm (4.7 inches) in diameter, and weighs 48 kg (106 pounds). The inboard wing pylon is armed with a radar-guided R-3R (NATO designation AA-2-2 Atoll) AAM. The R-3R is 3350mm (131.9 inches) long, 127mm (5 inches) in diameter, and weighs 90 kg (198 pounds). (Stephan Boshniakov)

This *Voenno Vozdushnye Sili* (VVS; Soviet Air Force) MiG-21*bis Lazur* (White 73) has a UB-32 rocket pod on the inboard wing pylon and a UB-16-57U rocket pod on the outboard pylon. These pods each hold thirty-two and sixteen 57mm unguided rockets, respectively. The Light Gray undersurface camouflage is most unusual for Soviet MiG-21s, which normally had Pale Blue undersurfaces. Upper surfaces were painted Olive Green and Tan, while the tactical number on the nose is a thin White outline against the camouflage. (Sergej F. Sergejev)

Two R-60M AAMs are mounted on an APU-60-IIM double launcher fitted to this BVVS MiG-21*bis Lazur*'s outboard wing pylon. This missile has a range of approximately 20 km (12.4 miles). An APU-13MT missile rail mounted on the inboard wing pylon carries an Infrared (IR) homing R-3S (NATO designation AA-2 Atoll) AAM. The older R-3S is 2838mm (111.7 inches) long, with a diameter of 127mm, weighs 73.5 kg (162 pounds), and has a range of 12 km (7.5 miles). (Stephan Boshniakov)

The MiG-21*bis* SAU has the RSBN-5S ILS antenna mounted on the tailfin immediately above the conical SOD-57M Air Traffic Control (ATC) transponder antenna. The RSBN-5S was not mounted on the earlier MiG-21*bis Lazur*. A Red covering protects the tripole SRO-2 *Khrom* (Odd Rods) IFF antenna just ahead of the ILS antenna. (Harald Ziewe)

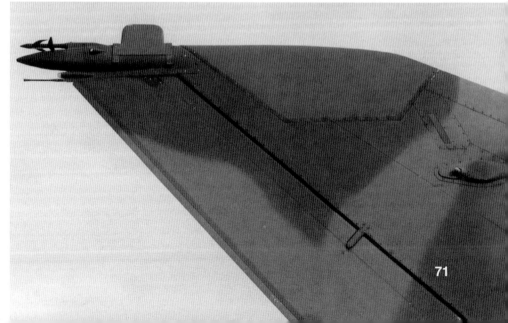

This natural metal MiG-21SM (Red 22) was assigned to a *Voenno Vozdushnye Sili* (VVS; Soviet Air Force) Fighter Aviation Regiment in August of 1968. Two Red bands on the aft fuselage identified VVS aircraft that supported the Warsaw Pact invasion of Czechoslovakia on 20-21 August 1968.

The Silakh al-Jawwiya as-Sudaniya (Sudanese Air Force) operated this MiG-21M (Black 345) during 1979. The Fishbed J's tactical number was painted in both Arabic and English numerals on the nose and rear fuselage.

This *Al Quwwat al-Jawwia il-Misriya* (Egyptian Air Force) MiG-21M (Black 8212) was retrofitted with a TS-27AMSh rear view mirror in the canopy. It participated in BRIGHT STAR 83, a joint US-Egyptian military exercise held in Egypt in August of 1983. The Fishbed J is camouflaged with Egyptian Medium Green (approximately FS34159) and Sand (approx. FS33564) upper surfaces and Pale Blue (approx. FS35450) undersurfaces.

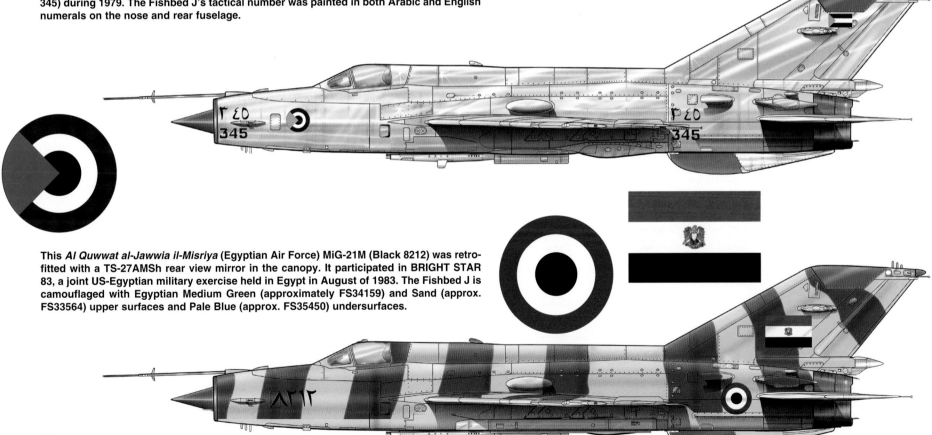

The VVS deployed this MiG-21MF (Red 27) to Afghanistan early in the 1979-88 Soviet-Afghan War. Four Red stars painted under the canopy were mission tally marks. The Soviets camouflaged this Fishbed J with Earth Brown (approx. FS20140) and Tan (approx. FS20400) upper surfaces and Pale Blue undersurfaces. This MiG-21MF later served as a Ukrainian Air Force instructional airframe coded Red 127.

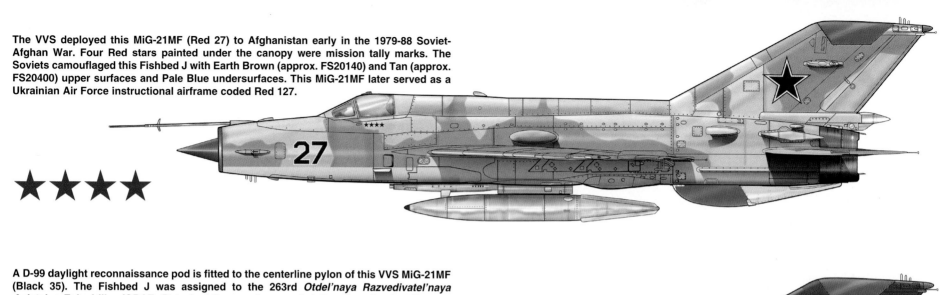

A D-99 daylight reconnaissance pod is fitted to the centerline pylon of this VVS MiG-21MF (Black 35). The Fishbed J was assigned to the 263rd *Otdel'naya Razvedivatel'naya Aviatsiya Eskadril'ya* (ORAE: Detached Reconnaissance Aviation Squadron) at Bagram Air Base near Kabul, Afghanistan in 1983. Its upper surfaces are painted Green (approx. FS34062), Medium Green (approx. FS24172), and Tan, while the undersurfaces are Pale Blue. Three Hero of the Soviet Union medals are painted as mission tallies on the nose.

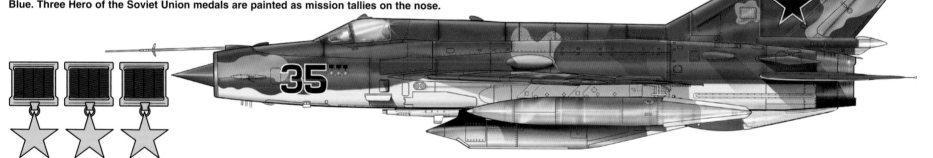

The 4th Aviation Squadron of the VVS Aviation Academy flew this MiG-21MF (Red 117) in 1991. The Academy was located at Chuguev Air Base near Kharkov, Ukraine. An eye was painted just aft of the radome, while a sailing ship appeared under the windshield. VVS aircraft assigned to training units had three-digit tactical numbers, while aircraft in combat units had two-digit numbers. Aircraft colors are Green and Earth Brown over Light Gray (approx. FS26496)

Two Red bands are pained on the aft fuselage of this *Voenno Vozdushnye Sili* (VVS: Soviet Air Force) MiG-21SM (Red 22). These bands identified Soviet aircraft that support-ed the invasion of the *Ceskoslovenska Socialisticka Republica* (CSSR; Czechoslovak Socialist Republic) on 20-21 August 1968. This invasion by Soviet, Polish, East German, Hungarian, and Bulgarian troops ended the 'Prague Spring' of reforms led by Czechoslovak Communist Party leader Alexander Dubcek. An APU-7D launching rail for the RS-2US (NATO designation AA-1 Alkali) AAM was mounted on the inboard wing pylon. (Nicholas J. Waters III)

This *Al Quwwat al-Jawwia il-Misriya* (Egyptian Air Force) MiG-21M participated in exercise BRIGHT STAR 83 held in Egypt during August of 1983. The TS-27AMSh rear view mirror was retrofitted during the course of its operational service. An APU-13 missile rail is mounted on the inboard wing pylon. This carried the R-3S (AA-2 Atoll) AAM. The Black tactical number 8212 is invisible against the second Medium Green band aft of the nose. (Dick Cole/Cole Aero Graphics)

Three 490 L (129-gallon) auxiliary fuel tanks are mounted on this *Letectvo Ceskoslovenske Lidove Armady* (LCLA; Czechoslovak People's Army Air Force) MiG-21M (Black 1203). These tanks were mounted on the centerline fuselage and the outboard wing pylons. This fuel tank configuration was only used on long-range ferry flights, since this degraded combat maneuverability. The external tanks' combined 1470 L (388 gallons) supplement-ed the 2600 L (687-gallon) internal fuel capacity. The first MiG-21M was delivered to the LCLA during 1969. (Zdenek Hurt)

Another participant in BRIGHT STAR 83 was this *Silakh al-Jawwiya as-Sudaniya* (Sudanese Air Force) MiG-21M (Black 345). The tactical number painted on the nose and the rear fuselage was in Arabic and English style numerals. All three air brakes were fully deployed and the air intake covered. The cockpit access ladder was standard for Soviet and foreign Fishbeds. (Nicholas J. Waters III)

Several VVS MiG-21MFs are lined up at a Soviet air base. Soviet Fishbed Js were originally delivered in natural metal. The second and third MiG-21MFs each display the Red *Otlitshnij Samoljot* (Excellent Aircraft Award) emblem on the nose. The pilots wear ZSh-3 helmets and carry KM-32 oxygen masks. (Andrzej Morgala)

A derelict *Dayuuradaha Xoogga Dalka Somaliyeed* (DXDS; Somali Aeronautical Corps) MiG-21MF (Blue 252/Serial Number 8901) rests at Mogadishu Air Base, Somalia in December of 1992. US troops painted the Red lettering AFEOD (Air Force Explosive Ordinance Disposal) under the air data boom platform on this Fishbed's nose. The Americans were tasked with restoring order before handing over control to the United Nations. The Soviet Union delivered the first seven of approximately 40 MiG-21MFs to the DXDS in July of 1974. (Paul A. Jackson)

An eye is painted ahead of the tactical number of this Soviet MiG-21MF (Red 117). A sailing ship is painted aft of this number. The MiG-21MF was assigned to the 4. *Eskadrilya Aviatsionnaya* (Aviation Squadron), VVS Academy at Chuguev Air Base near Kharkov, Ukrainian Soviet Socialist Republic (now Ukraine). Three-digit tactical numbers were exclusively issued to VVS training units, while operational units had two-digit tactical numbers. (Sergej F. Sergejev)

A natural metal *Polskie Wojska Lotnicze* (PWL; Polish Air Force) MiG-21MF (Red 8006/Serial Number 968006) taxis either before or after a training mission in 1990. It was assigned to the 2. *Pulk Lotnictwa Mysliwskiego 'Krakow'* (PLM; Fighter Aviation Regiment 'Cracow') at Goleniow. This Fishbed J is armed with a UB-16-57U pod (sixteen 57MM S-5 unguided rockets) on the inboard pylon and a 50 KG (110-pound) FAB-50 practice bomb on the outer wing pylon. The PWL disbanded the 2. PLM *'Krakow'* in 1993, due to Polish defense budget cutbacks. (Wojciech Luczak)

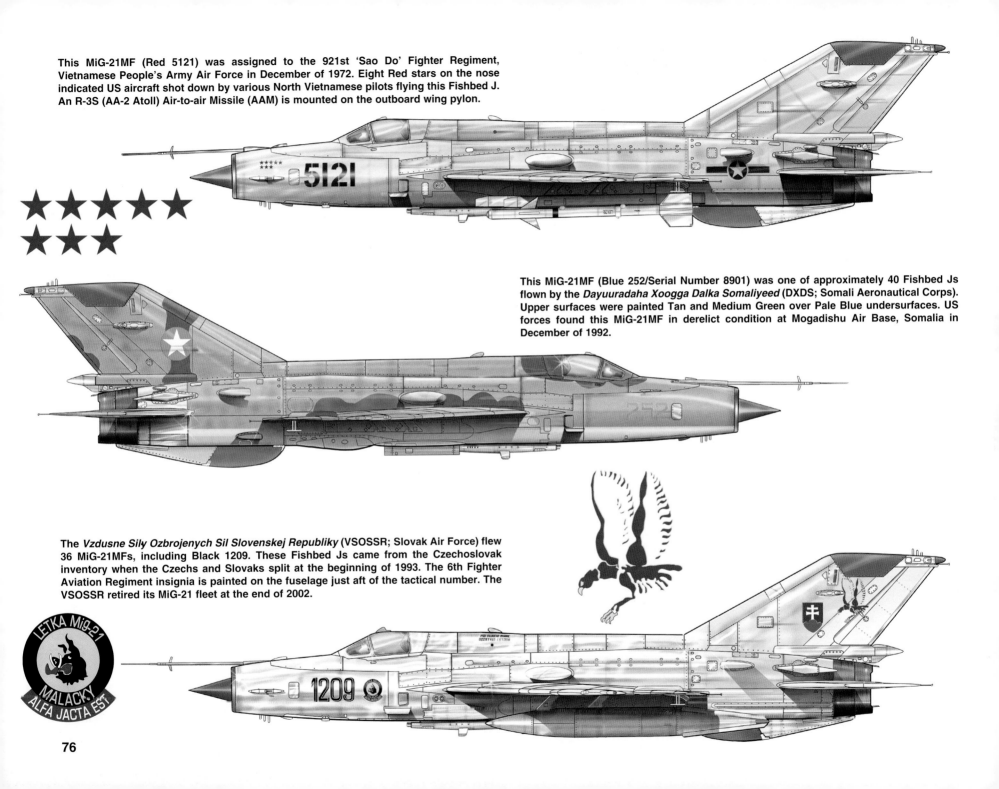

This MiG-21MF (Red 5121) was assigned to the 921st 'Sao Do' Fighter Regiment, Vietnamese People's Army Air Force in December of 1972. Eight Red stars on the nose indicated US aircraft shot down by various North Vietnamese pilots flying this Fishbed J. An R-3S (AA-2 Atoll) Air-to-air Missile (AAM) is mounted on the outboard wing pylon.

This MiG-21MF (Blue 252/Serial Number 8901) was one of approximately 40 Fishbed Js flown by the *Dayuuradaha Xoogga Dalka Somaliyeed* (DXDS; Somali Aeronautical Corps). Upper surfaces were painted Tan and Medium Green over Pale Blue undersurfaces. US forces found this MiG-21MF in derelict condition at Mogadishu Air Base, Somalia in December of 1992.

The *Vzdusne Sily Ozbrojenych Sil Slovenskej Republiky* (VSOSSR; Slovak Air Force) flew 36 MiG-21MFs, including Black 1209. These Fishbed Js came from the Czechoslovak inventory when the Czechs and Slovaks split at the beginning of 1993. The 6th Fighter Aviation Regiment insignia is painted on the fuselage just aft of the tactical number. The VSOSSR retired its MiG-21 fleet at the end of 2002.

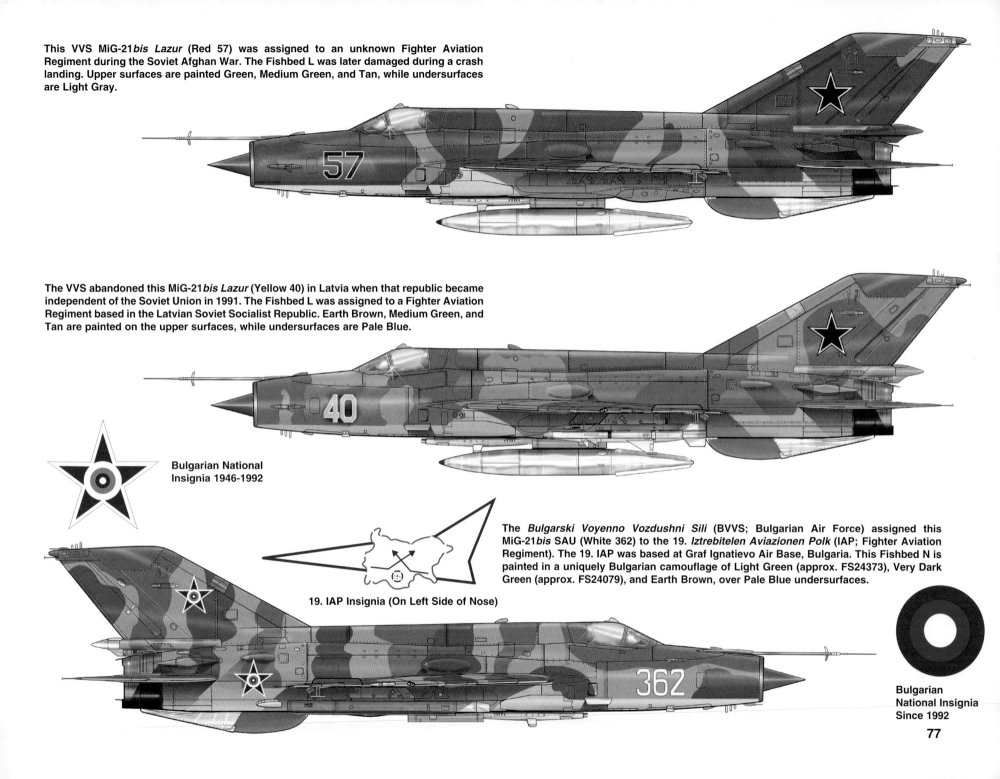

This VVS MiG-21*bis Lazur* (Red 57) was assigned to an unknown Fighter Aviation Regiment during the Soviet Afghan War. The Fishbed L was later damaged during a crash landing. Upper surfaces are painted Green, Medium Green, and Tan, while undersurfaces are Light Gray.

The VVS abandoned this MiG-21*bis Lazur* (Yellow 40) in Latvia when that republic became independent of the Soviet Union in 1991. The Fishbed L was assigned to a Fighter Aviation Regiment based in the Latvian Soviet Socialist Republic. Earth Brown, Medium Green, and Tan are painted on the upper surfaces, while undersurfaces are Pale Blue.

Bulgarian National
Insignia 1946-1992

19. IAP Insignia (On Left Side of Nose)

The *Bulgarski Voyenno Vozdushni Sili* (BVVS; Bulgarian Air Force) assigned this MiG-21*bis* SAU (White 362) to the 19. *Iztrebitelen Aviazionen Polk* (IAP; Fighter Aviation Regiment). The 19. IAP was based at Graf Ignatievo Air Base, Bulgaria. This Fishbed N is painted in a uniquely Bulgarian camouflage of Light Green (approx. FS24373), Very Dark Green (approx. FS24079), and Earth Brown, over Pale Blue undersurfaces.

Bulgarian
National Insignia
Since 1992

A *Letectvo Ceskoslovenske Armady* (LCA; Czechoslovak Army Air Force) MiG-21MF (Black 7713/Serial Number 967713) is about to touch down concluding a mission. All three speed brakes are deployed. APU-13MT missile rails were mounted on the outboard wing pylons, while APU-7 missile rails are fitted to the inboard wing pylons. This Fishbed J was transferred to the newly formed *Vzdusne Sily Ozbrojenych Sil Slovenskej Republiky* (VSOSSR; Slovak Air Force) on 1 January 1993. (Sign via Roman Sekyrka)

The newly formed VSOSSR (Slovak Air Force) absorbed this former *Letectvo Ceskoslovenske Armady* (LCA; Czechoslovak Army Air Force) MiG-21MF (Black 7713/Serial Number 967713) into service on 1 January 1993. The Slovak Republic operated 36 MiG-21MFs after the Slovaks and Czechs split up. The camouflage and tactical number were left unchanged, but the new Slovak national markings were added to the tail and wings. The entire Slovak MiG-21 fleet was phased out of service in late 2002. (Marcus Fülber)

Maintenance is performed on this *Luftstreitkräfte der Nationalen Volksarmee* (LSK NVA; East German Air Force) MiG-21MF (Red 513/Serial Number 8613) in August of 1984. It was assigned to *Jagdfliegergeschwader* (JG; Fighter Aviation Regiment) 3 *'Wladimir Komarow'* at Preschen. A Red 1 was painted in front of the actual tactical number to confuse Western analysts. The German Democratic Republic (GDR, or East Germany) commonly practiced this deception on publicly released photographs. (Hans-Joachim Mau)

This former East German MiG-21MF (Red 513/Serial Number 8613) received the West German inventory number 23+17. *Wehrtechnische Dienststelle* (WTD; Flight Test Evaluation Center) 61 of the *Bundesluftwaffe* (Federal German Air Force) evaluated this Fishbed J after German reunification in 1990. These tests were performed at WTD 61's home at Manching Air Base near Ingolstadt, Bavaria, Germany. (Harald Ziewe)

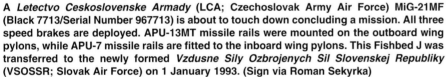

This MiG-21*bis Lazur* (Yellow 40) was assigned to a Fighter Aviation Regiment that was based in the former Latvian Soviet Socialist Republic. Latvia became independent in September of 1991 and forced the VVS (Soviet Air Force) to close its bases in this Baltic Republic. The Soviets left MiG-21s of several variants behind upon their withdrawal. The newly formed Latvian Air Force did not adopt the MiG-21 into its inventory. This MiG-21*bis* still carries a radar homing R-3R (NATO designation AA-2-2 Atoll) Air-to-Air Missile (AAM) on the outboard wing pylon and an RS-2US (NATO designation AA-1 Alkali) beam riding AAM on the inboard wing pylon. (Marcus Fülber)

Two *Hratsko Ratno Zrakoplovstvo* (HRZ; Croatian Air Force) MiG-21*bis Lazurs* fly with a pair of United States Air Force (USAF) Lockheed Martin F-16 Fighting Falcons over the Adriatic Coast. Both Croatian Fishbed Ls are flying 'clean' – without any external loads – while the F-16s each have a fuel tank on the centerline pylon and AIM-9 Sidewinder AAMs on the wingtips. (Croatian Ministry of Defense)

An *Ilmavoimat* (Finnish Air Force) MiG-21*bis Lazur* (MG-122/Serial Number 75084145) is parked at Utti Air Base, Finland in May of 1981. This MiG-21*bis Lazur* – assigned to *Hävittäjälentolaivue* (HävLLv; Fighter Squadron) 31 at Kuopio-Rissala – was lost on 22 March 1995. Smaller national markings and tactical numbers were adopted during the 1980s. HävLLv 31's Black lynx insignia was painted on the tail. The *Ilmavoimat* retired its MiG-21*bis Lazurs* in March of 1998 and HävLLv 31 converted to the Boeing (McDonnell Douglas) F/A-18C Hornet. (Klaus Niska)

This MiG-21*bis* SAU (White 362/Serial Number 75094362) was assigned to the 19. *Iztrebitelen Aviazionen Polk* (IAP; Fighter Aviation Regiment), *Bulgarski Voyenno Vozdushni Sili* (BVVS; Bulgarian Air Force). This Regiment was based at Graf Ignatievo, near Plovdiv in western Bulgaria. The Fishbed N has the post-Communist Bulgarian national marking that was introduced in 1992. A unit insignia is painted in front of the tactical number. The BVVS later redesignated the 19. IAP as the 3. *Iztrebitelna Aviazionna Basa* (IAB; Fighter Aviation Base), which is still based at Graf Ignatievo. This MiG-21*bis* SAU crashed on 16 May 2003. (Stephan Boshniakov)

Fox Two!
More Combat Jets from squadron/signal publications

5501 F-16 Fighting Falcon

5518 F/A-18 Hornet

5523 F-105 Thunderchief

5526 F-117 Nighthawk

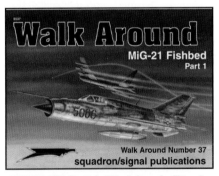

5537 MiG-21 Fishbed, Pt. 1

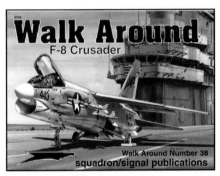

5538 F-8 Crusader

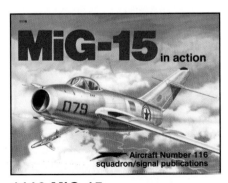

1116 MiG-15

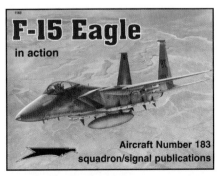

1183 F-15 Eagle

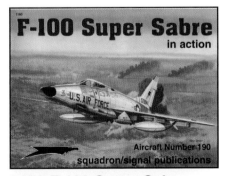

1190 F-100 Super Sabre

For more information on squadron/signal books, visit www.squadron.com